"NEVER THINK ABOUT YESTERDAY

...or worry about tomorrow."

The Life and Times of Gene Benedetti

by Douglas Pricer

For information contact::

Douglas Pricer • 8782 Sailport • Huntington Beach, California 92648

Email: dpricer@aol.com

Published by Christopher Brown – Garza Industries, Inc. Orange, California.

ISBN #0-9712615-1-2

To Gene and Evie

Alla Mia Cara,

Tu Figlioccio,

Doug

ACKNOWLEDGEMENTS

John Donne once wrote that "no man is an island". Since he did a lot of writing, he also knew that no writer writes alone. And so it is with this book. None of it could have happened without the help of many. To all listed here and to those I inadvertently missed I am sincerely grateful.

A special thanks to my old Danish friend Claus Jessen for his guidance, his skillful editing and great photography.

To Rear Admiral James Grealish USNR (Ret.) and USF class of '42, for his almost total recall of San Francisco as it was back in the day, his patience in sharing it with me and his steady encouragement. This could not have been done without Jim!

Gene's Navy pal and fellow Tunney Fish, Jim Bligh was essential to this work. His stories and sense of humor were like taking a trip back in time and I will be forever grateful.

A hearty thanks to Father Michael Kotlanger S.J. Father Michael is the archivist at USF and was an endless source of knowledge, an eternal optimist and an all around great guy.

To Tom Corbett; "Touchdown Tommy" is a proud mission kid, a San Francisco historian, a lifelong brother and a Poly Parrot till he dies.

A special thanks to Gen. Richard Hearney USMC (Ret.) for helping to acquire military records and saving months of time.

My heartfelt thanks to Rockette, Ida and Rose Pirro for their willingness to share family pictures and tell old stories that were at times painful.

To all the old time USF footballers, including Joe Clerou, Charlie White, Vic Ramus, and Bob St. Clair for their great stories. Big thanks as well too Milt Vuninich of Stanford University class of '43 for his wonderful account of the 1940 Stanford vs. USF game and to Blondy Black's roommate, Larmar Blount Mississippi State class of '43, for his fantastic storyies of the MSC vs. USF game in 1941.

To every Leghorn who ever wore the Blue and Gold and to every Leggie fan who heard the screech of *Leviticus* ascend into the Petaluma sky. And to Paul Halverson and all the kids in the *No Fair* Gang who hopped the fence at Durst Field and watched it all.

A very special thanks to June Burtner (PHS class of '38) for her wonderful accounts of the Leggies and the great pictures she provided.

To all of Gene's friends who told their stories including Duke Iverson, Jim Leprino, Stiney Stienbeck, Bob Acrone, Jack Dei, Bud Chadwick, Fran Burke, Joe Clerou, Don Ramatici and of course the irrepressible *Peopleologist*, Bill Soberanes.

Many thanks are due to Gary and Lynn Imm for their patience and time.

The archival departments at Sports Illustrated, the University of San Francisco, the University of Norte Dame, Hardin Simmons University, Mississippi State University, Santa Clara University, Catholic University, Santa Rosa Junior College and Petaluma High School librarian Nancy Sieck. All were essential to this effort.

My thanks also to writer and patriot John Barry Dwyer author of *Scouts and Raiders*, Ens. L.L. Culver (USNR), for his heartfelt account of Cus Pirros' story and to Ben Salata of the UDT – SEAL Museum at Ft. Pierce, FL for their help.

Very special thanks to Chris Brown and Sharon Swaagstra – two colleagues and friends for their help in the entire process.

The entire Benedetti and Libarle families – good Lord did they all show patience!

To my kids; Zachariah, Tina, Jeremiah, Courtney, Casey and "Goo Pa's" boy Bryce, for lighting my life.

And finally to my long suffering, steadfast and loving wife Shelley for putting up with a husband like me. God bless them all.

PREFACE

This is a book about the life and times of Gene Benedetti. It is a book about what it was like and how it felt to live in America as the son of Italian immigrants from the early decades of the twentieth century to the present day.

Because this book is a biography, it is presented against the backdrop of history. But in a greater sense it is much more because the stories told herein are recounted in Genes' own words and in the words of those who know him. And in describing those times, in reminiscing about his days in college, in recalling his adventures and sacrifices in the worst catastrophe in world history and his life afterward, it brings to life with sharp impact the circumstances and passions of an era that can never return.

With no apologies to the non-fan there is a lot of football in this book. Football, as it was played in Gene's day, was a primary source for the toughness and perseverance along with the rich sense of humor that characterizes his personality.

But more than anything this is a book about family. It is about a humble man who loves his wife and children, remains steadfast to his friends, is forever proud of his heritage and is fiercely patriotic to his country.

It is a great story. I hope I have given it the book it deserves.

Doug Pricer
Huntington Beach, California
October 2003

PROLOGUE

In January 2000 my best friend, Dan Benedetti, asked me to write the story of his uncle Dante, a Marine aviator, who was killed in 1942 while flying a combat mission in the South Pacific skies over Guadalcanal. Dante's body was never recovered and the pain associated with his tragic death has remained with his family since. In the course of my research, I found two of Dante's surviving squadron mates, one of whom, by a miraculous coincidence, flew on his wing on the morning of his death and was able to tell me how he died, thus solving a mystery that had lingered in the family for nearly sixty years. The publication of Dante's story, entitled The Last Plane Up, resulted in his posthumous induction, along with his brother Gene (my Godfather) and his sister, Milli, into a World War Two flyers club in Santa Rosa, California in February 2001.

As the author, and a friend of the family, I was asked to come to Santa Rosa and say a few words at the induction ceremony. Addressing such a group was a deep honor for me. As I stood to speak and looked into the eyes of these aging heroes who had helped save our nation and, indeed, the world, I was overwhelmed with a sincere sense of humility and gratitude. At one table sat the man who flew as a navigator on the scout plane that spotted the Japanese fleet at the historic battle of Midway. At another, an old fighter pilot who had served in Europe. At still another, my Godfather, Gene Benedetti, a hero who served with distinction and valor, survived to return home, marry, raise six children, start a professional football team, found a successful business, and live to enjoy the warm security of the freedom that he and his brother had purchased with their courage, and in Dante's case, his life.

After the ceremony, Gene and I drove back to the family home in the foothills overlooking the town of Cotati. It was a beautiful winter day, cold and clear, as we turned off Poplar Avenue onto the narrow macadam road that leads to the circular driveway in front of the large country home. We stepped out of the car, and my Godfather walked me over to the edge of the driveway to the base of a huge eucalyptus tree. Spread below us in the sparkling valley lay the contrasting towns of Cotati and Rohnert Park; the former pre-dating the Civil War and the latter a result of a 1960's real estate boom that had consumed the Rohnert family's enormous seed farm.

"You know," my Godfather said, as he puffed on his pipe. "When I was a kid, I used to climb up this hill and sit in the shade under this tree. I'd look out across the valley at Sonoma Mountain and off in the distance to Mt. St. Helena and dream about building a big house up here." Then he turned and looked at the house and smiled. "Come on", he said as he put his arm around me. "Let's go inside."

Inside the house was cool and quiet. "Let's have a drink, Buck," he said. I walked over to the far corner of the sprawling family room and stepped behind the bar. I took my time mixing the drinks, putting in a handful of ice and spearing several olives on a plastic toothpick before I poured the Bombay and added the lemon twist. "Here's cheers," he said as he raised his glass. "It's good to have you back, Buck."

"It's good to be back," I answered as we sat down at the old wooden table next to the kitchen.

We sat together for several hours, eating bread and cheese and drinking gin. As always I felt comfortable and accepted. As the afternoon passed, we talked and laughed about all that had happened over the last thirty years.

"Evie and I always thought of you as one of our sons," he chuckled. "The only mistake I made was not whipping your ass earlier."

"Yeah," I agreed. "You probably should have." And then we laughed and had another drink.

Outside, the sun dropped behind the coastal mountains, and turned the emerald shades of the valley to a deep purple dusk. As my Godfather rose to light a fire in the old brick fireplace, I was suddenly struck by the enormity of this humble man and the uniqueness of his life.

Later that evening, he and his wife Evie gathered the family for dinner around the big table in the family room. Before we began, my Godfather smiled at his youngest daughter Gina and asked her to offer a blessing. With her little boy Coulter sitting on her lap and the crackling fire casting a warm and comforting glow, we joined hands and bowed our heads. "Bless us O' Lord," the young mother prayed softly and then recited the simple prayer of thanks that has preceded every meal at the family table for nearly four generations. When we finished I smiled up at my Godfather and squeezed his hand. "One day," I said to myself. "I'll write your story."

JUNE 6, 1944

Gene Benedetti.

I

It was cold and damp on the dull gray morning of June 6, 1944 as the Landing Craft Tanks (LCT) of Gunfire Support Group (GSG) Assault Group O -1 struggled through the rolling waters of the English Channel. Topside, in the pilothouse of LCT-210, Ensign Gene Benedetti strained as he peered shoreward through the wet gloom and tried to spot the church steeple located between the tiny villages of Colleville and Vierville that was his navigational landfall. Overhead, a thick mist hung like a damp shroud over his ship, and in the dull light of the breaking dawn the young officer shivered.

As he looked down through the sea splattered window of the wheelhouse, he could see his cargo of three 33-ton Sherman tanks sitting on their elevated platforms with their 75mm guns protruding over the bow ramp. Clustered amidships behind the tanks on the main deck, 140 combat engineers mingled nervously in the salty spray as they checked and rechecked their equipment and fought to stave off a gut wrenching seasickness as the flat-bottom craft slewed about in the rough seas. Despite the fact that he was just five months shy of his twenty-fifth birthday, Benedetti was a seasoned combat veteran, having seen action at Oran and Algeria in North Africa, and later at the invasions of Sicily, Salerno, and bloody Anzio. He had been in the Navy since May of 1942 when he had enlisted during the spring of his senior year at the University of San Francisco.

Behind and all around him the largest invasion force in the history of the world, comprised of 4,000 invasion ships, 600 war ships, 10,000 planes and more than 175,000 Allied troops surged toward the coast of France. Their mission was to invade Europe, defeat the German army, purge the continent of its Nazi slave masters and ultimately, to save the world.

"Our group commander, Captain Lorenzo Sabin, told us we had nothing to worry about," Benedetti ruefully recalled nearly sixty years later. "You'll be heading into a 'dead beach' Gene," he said. "Our planes and rockets will bomb the hell out of them. The Germans will either be gone, dead or caught by surprise. It'll be no problem."

But as the savvy young officer looked through the mist at the beach code named Omaha, he had his doubts. Years later, historians would describe the assault at Omaha beach as a heroic call to glory. But as the careening LCT's approached the waterline and the first red tracers from the German 88's thundered through the air, the horrified young skipper knew at once that Captain Sabin and the other planners had been sorely mistaken.

Sonoma California 1919

Giacondo and Pia Benedetti on their wedding day in Convalle, Italy.

II

"It was the morning train that brought you."

Pia Benedetti

Nestled amid the rolling green hills of Northern California's Valley of the Moon, there are few places richer in California history than the town of Sonoma. Indeed, it was here, just off the picturesque town square, that the brash and ambitious Father Jose Altamira established the last of California's famous missions when he planted the cross at mission San Francisco de Solano in 1823. And just twenty-three years later, on June 14, 1846, Sonoma hosted the Bear Flag Revolt, a twenty-five day uprising that led to California's admission to the Union.

With its mild climate, fertile valleys and lush green hills, the region was a natural draw for immigrants with farming experience. In 1857 a Hungarian nobleman and viticulturist named Agoston Haraszthy landed in town and established California's wine industry when he built the Buena Vista winery. Tucked beside a crystal stream the cave-like cellars and classic fieldstone buildings of the Buena Vista were a beautiful setting and even today remain a popular attraction for visitors.

Haraszthy was not the only winemaker to settle in Sonoma. Arriving from the Italian province of Tuscany in 1895, Samuele Sebastaini brought his formidable farming and vintner skills to town. In 1904, after a humble start as a laborer, he acquired his own vineyards and began selling his wine by the cup to thirsty laborers from his horse-drawn cart. Today, after nearly a century of continuous operation, Sebastaini Family Vineyards continue to be one of America's leading producers of wines.

In 1915, Giacondo and Pia Benedetti arrived from their native Italy. Like the Sebastaini's, the couple hailed from the agricultural region of Tuscany and had come to America seeking a new life. After arriving in New York and being processed through Ellis Island, they had migrated by rail to San Francisco. They settled into an apartment on Green Street in the Italian enclave of North Beach to await the birth of their first child, Emily on January 4, 1914. However, Pia had not taken well to the cold and damp of The City and fearing pneumonia (a deadly condition in those days) her doctor recommended a warmer climate. As a result, the little family soon found themselves moving north to the warmer environs of Sonoma, where Giacondo rented a tiny house in the town's Italian section near the railroad tracks. Blessed with a gregarious enthusiasm and a strong work ethic, he soon found work in the local stone quarry cutting cobblestones for the streets of San Francisco. It was tough, dirty work, and it was here, in the dust and grit of the quarry, that the rugged immigrant met Sam Sebastiani's brother, Charlie. The two discovered that they were both from Tuscany and became fast friends. When Pia's second child Dante was born in November of 1915, it was Charlie's wife Rose, in her role as neighborhood midwife, who delivered him.

Four years later, on a cold winter evening, Rose once again was summoned to the modest house by the tracks to sit through the night with her friend. As the sun finally rose in the eastern sky, the two women heard the shriek of a train whistle pierce the frigid dawn, and felt the little house tremble as the great string of steel and steam thundered by outside the window. The date was December 19, 1919, and Gene M. Benedetti had entered the world. Years later Pia would smile as she recalled that chilly morning and tell her youngest son. "It was the morning train that brought you."

EARLY YEARS

Gene's 3rd grade class at the Cotati School.
Gene is third row, third from right.

III

"I was milking cows at eight years old."

Gene Benedetti

By the time young Gene was born, WWI, the "War to End all Wars" was over. America, stunned by the catastrophic losses in Europe, not to mention over 300,000 casualties of her own, heaved a collective sigh of thanks and relief.

The free wheeling ethos that followed – dubbed by historians as "The Roaring Twenties" - characterized the nation's desire to "Just Live." And live it did, as Americans everywhere cast aside their puritan undergarments and kicked up their heels.

One of the most noteworthy changes in the twenties was the passage of the Eighteenth Amendment, the Volstead Act, prohibiting the manufacture, sale and distribution of alcoholic beverages. Despite its' intent, the law caused a backlash among Americans who turned to drinking illegal alcohol in record numbers. The results were a windfall of opportunity for criminals like Al Capone and others who soon turned America's cities into profit centers of free-wheeling corruption and crime.

But despite the negative aspects of prohibition, the 1920s proved to be a time of great cultural ferment in America. For example, in literature young writers like Ernest Hemingway and F. Scott Fitzgerald wrote epic novels like *The Sun Also Rises* and *The Great Gatsby*, respectively. And in 1930, a brilliant young author from Sauk Centre, Minnesota named Sinclair Lewis gave America its first Nobel Prize for literature.

On the nation's fields of play, men like Babe Ruth, Jack Dempsey, Red Grange and Bobby Jones became bigger-than-life as they defined "The Golden Age of Sports" and commanded huge salaries while performing before enormous crowds.

Out west, in a bustling little town called Hollywood, a new cinematic technology called the "talkie" took hold. Soon thereafter moviegoers all over America flocked to neighborhood theaters to plunk down a dime and watch the flickering images of actors like William Powell, Mary Pickford, and a former Jewish vaudeville singer named Al Jolson prophetically tell the country: "You ain't seen nothin' yet."

The 20s were also a time of remarkable technological achievement. In a decade often called the second industrial revolution, the nations manufacturing base, developed during the war, provided consumers with a host of new products designed to make daily life easier. As a result, appliances like vacuum cleaners were soon crawling out of housewives' closets, electric irons were sailing across starched shirts like little iron ships parting the seas, and the whirr of electric refrigerators were singing the death knell to ice men everywhere. The Ford Motor Company epitomized the revolution when its moving assembly line (invented by Ramson E. Olds) cranked out over 15 million Model T's, (customers could choose from any color as long as it was black), while paying workers the unheard wage of five dollars a day. By 1927 Ford's "Tin Lizzies" (so called because the car contained vanadium steel) and an ever increasing spider web of concrete highways were taking Americans to destinations they could only dream of a few years before. Inundated by an avalanche of advertising, and connected by a new electronic marvel called the radio, people everywhere were becoming more affluent as the nation began to develop a middle class of consumers.

While commonplace today, these developments changed the world for Americans in the 1920s and Sonoma County was no exception. Developed as a prime agricultural region in the mid nineteenth century, the county enjoyed a vigorous economy. The two major towns of Santa Rosa and Petaluma were both larger than average farming centers. As the county seat, Santa Rosa boasted a population of 8,750 citizens while about 6,000 people called Petaluma home. The primary income in the region came from fruit, hops, grapes, dairying, sheep and eggs. The wine industry was all but shut down during prohibition. The railroad connected the county, and provided some work for locals, but for the most part men farmed their own land or worked for others. The average laborer's wage for a ten-hour day was about $1.50. But in the 20s a loaf of bread cost a nickel, a trip to the movies was a dime, a new Ford could be purchased on credit for under $300.00 and Sears & Roebuck would sell "on time" from their catalog an 800 square foot house for $629.00 (some assembly required).

Giacondo and Pia were nothing if not frugal and for them life in America, while tough, was manageable. In the course of just fifteen years they had made friends, were blessed with three healthy children, were paying their bills and were convinced that America was indeed the land of their dreams. It was time to branch out and find a place to permanently settle down. With that in mind,

Giacondo looked ten miles south of Santa Rosa to the little town of Cotati.

Located at the southern end of Northern California's Santa Rosa plain, Cotati's heritage reaches deep into antiquity. Over two thousand years before the arrival of the first white man in 1827, a Native American tribe called the Miwok inhabited the entire valley. Characterized by their passive and peaceful nature, the Miwoks lived in small bands of about one hundred people and enjoyed an existence rich in culture as they hunted the green hills, gathered nuts and berries in the fertile valleys and fished the bountiful streams and coastal waters. A band called the Kota'ti lived on the spot where the present town is today and it was from their legendary leader, Chief Cotati, that the little hamlet drew its name.

In the years when California was a Spanish dominion, Cotati and its surrounding area was a 17,000-acre land grant called Rancho Cotate. The rancho was originally awarded to Capt. Juan Castaneda. However, Castaneda could not hold the property and in 1849 – the year of California's famous gold rush - Dr. Thomas Stokes Page acquired the enormous spread. The Page family ran cattle and sheep on the land. In 1870, when the railroad was completed, a wood and water stop was built and named Pages Station. In 1892, Dr. Page's youngest son formed the Cotati Land Company and began to sub-divide and sell the property. The town of Cotati was born.

When the Benedetti's arrived in 1928, the settlement boasted several churches, a downtown plaza, shops, a couple of automobile dealerships – with shiny new cars that must have dazzled the family - and the Cotati Hotel. Along with the railroad, the town was connected to the rest of the county by present day Petaluma Hill

Road, known then as the Hill Road, or High Road, that ran to and from Santa Rosa. The "West Road," (today's Stony Point Road) led to the Page ranch, and also past the front doors of a raucous road-house and tavern called the Washoe House.

Giacondo had his eye on a fourteen-acre parcel upon which a Finnish family named Lathi had once operated a resort called the Hillside Swimming Pool and Steam Baths. Complete with a sauna and steam baths, the resort boasted a large outdoor swimming pool that featured a twenty-foot slide, an indoor dance floor, a snack bar, private changing rooms and a number of small overnight guest cabins. The entire facility was quaintly tucked away in the foothills just outside town. It was a beautiful setting and, indeed, was a favorite destination for tourists from San Francisco who traveled up country to swim, take a sauna and bathe in the pristine crystal air.

But when Mr. Lathi's wife died, he fell upon hard times. Wrought with grief, the brooding Finn burned down his house, poured cement down his well and apparently committed suicide. It is not clear who actually took ownership of the property after his death, but it is known that when Giacondo decided to buy it, he borrowed $3500, which was an enormous sum in those days, from an Italian friend named Santero.

"My dad had not saved much cash," recalled Gene. "But he saw the ranch as a real opportunity. Hell, business was good and so he borrowed the money from old man Santero and we got to work." Only eight years old at the time, young Gene learned early about hard work.

"We all pitched in," he said. "My Dad had a Mr. Keat, who was a well driller and had drilled the original well, come over and re-drill the old well. It was a very good well and in fact is still in use today. Then one of Dad's friends, a man named Lindo Binchini - I'll never forget him, from Santa Rosa - tore down the old changing rooms around the pool. I was only eight years old but me and my brother Dan helped. My job was to pull the nails from the wood and stack it. My dad and Lindo used it to build the house."

This was no small feat. In 1928 there were no industry standards governing the lumber industry. Consequently, almost all lumber was custom cut and thus each structure was built differently.

"The place was a real hodgepodge," Gene recalled. "It was part redwood, part fir, and God knows what all. It was full of flaws. The wood was all different sizes. It looked terrible, but we put a thick coat of plaster over it and you couldn't tell."

But flawed or not, the house was a sturdy one and did the job. In fact, it is still occupied by Gene's nephew, Jeff Libarle, and his family.

"We were happy," said Gene. "There was a kitchen, a living room, a bedroom for Mom and Dad, a room for my sister and one for myself and my brother Dan to share."

"It was a wonderful house," affirmed Gene's sister Milli. "I had a room to myself and the boys shared one. We all worked and lived together. Dan and I were close and looked out for Gene. He was such a short little kid, we named him Shorty."

Family life quickly became busy as the ranch began to take shape with the acquisition of a couple of cows, several hogs, and the conversion of a few outbuildings into chicken houses.

"We worked all the time," recalls Gene. "I was milking cows at eight years old and helping my Dad with the chores. We all did. Everyone had to do their part. It was all we knew. We just all worked together and lived off the ranch."

But it was not the Ritz. "For the first few years we had no electricity, and no lights," laughed Gene. "We had lanterns and candles."

"The well gave us plenty of fresh water but there was no indoor plumbing. We had an outhouse; it was a two-holer, outside the house. We took a bath once a week. My mother would put the tub in the middle of the kitchen and heat the water on the stove. We'd take a bath right in the kitchen. Hell, we didn't know the difference. We didn't know what plumbing was. But we were happy. We'd never had anything like that before and it was a good life."

For the Benedettis, the purchase of their own land and home was the realization of a dream that started in 1909 when Giacondo traveled from his native village of Convalle in the hardscrabble Tuscan hills to the port city of Genoa where he boarded the British built double stack liner Regina d' Italia and crossed the vast Atlantic to New York. On that first visit, which lasted two years, he had worked as a laborer in the eastern Sierra town of Bishop and had seen with his own eyes the infinite opportunities that America held for a man like himself who sought a fair chance in life and an opportunity to achieve. Struck with a spirit of opportunism, and seeking the freedom that only America could provide, he had returned to Convalle to marry Pia and in 1913 had brought her to America. Now, after fifteen years, as he and his wife planted their feet in the rich and fertile soil of their own land, the dream that they both held so dear had come true. Nearly seventy-five years later, their grandson Dan summed up what that meant to this tough and determined couple from Tuscany.

"Those fourteen acres were everything to my grandparents," Dan said. "They thought differently than we do today. To them the land was not an investment, to be improved upon and then sold for a profit. To them it was a living entity. Their connection to it was inseparable. From it they could feed their family, make their living and sustain a feeling of self worth and pride."

Indeed, in the deepest of farming traditions, the couple had a personal and deep respect for the land itself.

"They were the original environmentalists," Dan went on. "They knew that if they took care of their land, rotated the crops, fertilized the soil, and cared for the animals, that it would take care of them. In that regard, I never remember them complaining that the work was too hard – never. For them, working the land was life itself. They respected it and loved it."

THE DEPRESSION

Giacondo and Pia, a tough and determined couple from Tuscany.

IV

"We never saw a dime of our money . . ."

Gene Benedetti

Despite their optimism and resourcefulness Giacondo and Pia, (like most of America) never saw the dark and fearful clouds of economic disaster roiling on the nation's horizon.

The events that caused the Great Depression to sweep across America in 1929 were many. In general, a top-heavy distribution of the nation's wealth, combined with severely inflated stock prices and corporate greed, caused the country's unregulated stock market to crash in October of that year. The result was a catastrophic nose-dive of the nation's economy that led to bank closures, severe inflation and widespread unemployment. History tends to depict great events like the Depression in its extremes. Hence, soup kitchens, scruffy men selling apples on street corners, smoky shanty town "Hoovervilles", long lines of broken men seeking work, the dust bowl, and the horribly desperate plight of the family Joad portrayed by John Steinbeck in his 1939 classic, *The Grapes of Wrath*, serve as our impression of those times.

To a great extent, all of these perceptions were true. But in a broader reality, the Depression affected people in different ways.

In fact, some people were not affected at all while others suffered greatly. Where a person lived played a great part in defining their experience. For example, Jim Grealish was born "South of the Slot" (an area known today as SOMA or south of Market Street) and grew up in the Irish Mission district of San Francisco. He was twelve years old in 1932 when the depression was in full swing. Now a retired Naval Admiral, Jim has vivid memories of his life in The City during those years.

"My dad had come from Ireland in 1914," he recalled. "He worked down on the waterfront. Every morning they had what was called "The Shape Up". All of the men would go down to the waterfront looking for work and the foreman would pick out the guys that he needed for that day. If you got picked, you worked; if not, you didn't. I can remember many mornings when I was leaving for school and my dad was returning home from "The Shape Up" after not being picked."

"The church sent food baskets around and put them on people's front porches," Grealish went on. "But my dad was too proud for that. 'There'll be no baskets on our porch,' he'd intone. And there never was."

Despite the general depiction of chaos and despair, the Great Depression galvanized many communities. For instance, in May of 1934 there was a bitter maritime strike on San Francisco's waterfront. The violent shut down lasted for three months, reaching its peak when California governor Frank F. Merriam called out the National Guard, posted armed sentries on street corners and declared marshal law.

The discontent stretched beyond the waterfront and reached into the very fabric of the neighborhood's culture.

"In those days there was no such thing as strike benefits," explained Grealish. "There was no health insurance or anything like that. The strike lasted for three months and no one had any money. The neighborhood grocery store carried many families until the strike was over and the men could get back to work. That meant that the store's suppliers had to carry them, so you can see that everyone just pitched in and helped."

"But I never remember any thought of giving up," he continued. "Everyone helped each other. That's just the way it was."

In contrast to Grealish's plight, those living on farms, like the Benedetti's, had a different experience.

Gene remembers: "We never saw a dime of our money," he recalled. "In fact, my Dad never paid a cent towards the principal on the ranch during the entire depression, and he was always way behind on the feed bill."

"But," he continued, "we were never hungry. My mother was a fantastic cook. Some friends of my dad had built an oval shaped brick oven out in the yard and mom would bake Italian bread in it twice a week. She'd start a fire in it until it was blazing hot and then remove the coals and ash. The brick would hold the heat and she would put in loaves of bread and bake them in the oven. In the morning, on the days that she was baking bread, she'd take the fresh slabs of excess dough and make it into a circle and deep-fry it like a doughnut. Then she would roll it in sugar and that would be our breakfast – it was great!"

"My mom and dad gave a lot of food away," he went on. "We had everything. All of our vegetables came from my mother's garden. We slaughtered a couple of hogs every year and maybe a cow. Of course we had plenty of chickens and eggs. In the morning my mother would gather the eggs and clean and grade them by weight and make sure there were no cracks in them. She'd hold them up to a light and "candle" them to be sure that they were not fertile. When the egg man came around, she'd sell them for a little money."

"We were pretty much self-sustained," he continued. "We'd milk the cows every day. We'd separate the milk with a hand crank separator. The skim milk was fed to the pigs. My Mom made butter and cheese from the cream. My Dad also made salami and sausage and even his own prosciutto. He'd cure the ham with salt and pepper and then press it between two boards weighted down with a big rock."

And, of course, Giacondo made his famous wine.

"You could go out and pick grapes for free," smiled Gene. "The government allowed two hundred gallons per family but we always made more. Anyone who came over always left with wine, or bread, or cheese or whatever we had. It was the way it was; everyone just helped any way they could."

Along with its natural bounty the ranch progressed technologically.

"After about three years, we got electricity," laughed Gene. "You had to qualify for it by having three appliances that ran on electricity. Dad changed the gas water pump to electric, and replaced thc old icebox with a used refrigerator. He also bought an electric separator for the milk. That qualified us and they ran electricity to the house. We were really living then!"

But overall, the depression years were extremely difficult. As the 1930's ground on, farming prices continued to bottom out, and the family lived on the margin of ruin.

"My dad couldn't make the ranch go," remembered Gene, "so he had to work out, (take outside jobs). He'd take his wagon and do hauling for people. It was one of the old "bottom dump" wagons with slats that were removable so what ever was in the wagon would dump out of the bottom."

"He was severely in debt." Gene went on. "He owed old man Santero for the note on the ranch and he also owed about $3800 to Everett Feed on the feed bill. In those days if you couldn't make the feed payment, the feed store took your land. Luckily, they knew my dad and didn't take our land. Dan and I and my sister helped my mother with the chores and dad was gone a lot. Sometimes he was gone for days at a time because he was working harvesting crops or doing general labor for other people."

HIGH SCHOOL

Petaluma High School, circa 1938

V

"We thought it was a beautiful campus ..."

June Burtner P.H.S. class of 1938

By the fall of 1935 the scene at the Benedetti household had changed. After graduating from high school, Gene's older sister Milli had enrolled at St. Luke's Hospital School of Nursing in San Francisco, while older brother Dante had moved away to college at Santa Clara University (he later transferred to USF). It was now Gene's turn to start high school. Taking the lead from his older siblings, he chose to commute ten miles south to the town of Petaluma.

Like its neighboring town of Cotati, Petaluma (incorporated in 1858), traces its history to the ancient Miwoks. In fact, the name Petaluma is a Miwok word meaning "flat hills" or "valley of flat hills." In 1834, as part of New Spain, General Mariano Vallejo established the first European settlement in the valley where the town now resides. By 1850, hunters, farmers, and trappers were camping in the area and trading goods with merchants in San Francisco via the Petaluma Creek (so called until 1959 when it was officially granted full river status). The town claims historical distinction in several areas. For example in the 1880's California's third rail line was built in Petaluma. And, in 1911 when a man named Fred J. Wiseman flew his mechanically-challenged aircraft all the way to Santa Rosa, a less than efficient demonstration that took two days to complete, (he could have walked it up there in less time), the town became home to the nation's first air mail flight.

But without doubt, Petaluma's greatest claim to fame originated in 1879 when Lyman C. Byce invented the first practical chicken incubator. Byce's invention opened the area to the poultry industry and by the late 1800's Petaluma was the largest center for poultry in the nation. At its peak, the town produced over 50 million dozen eggs annually. Under the capable proprietorship of one J.E. Keyes, Petaluma featured the world's only pharmacy dedicated to the health of the chicken. With civic events like National Egg Day, the Egg Queen Ball and the Chicken Rodeo, Petaluma grew to be the county's richest town and was known internationally as "The World's Egg Basket."

In 1873 the town also progressed academically when citizens purchased the community's first high school. Built in 1832 among the grand houses on 'D' street (on the site now occupied by the A. F. Tomasini home) the splendid wooden structure originally housed a private academy operated by Colonel J. D. Lippit. In 1886, an expanding student body of sixty-five pupils called for a larger building, and the campus was relocated to an impressive two-story dwelling on Liberty Street. Sitting atop the hill overlooking the entire valley, the location soon became known as "High School Hill." Twenty years later, local architect Brainerd Jones designed two handsome two-story buildings (one for the junior high school) on the present-day site on Fair Street. With the athletic fields (now Durst Field, named in honor of the all but forgotten

Superintendent of Instruction, David M. Durst) in the rear of the property, the new campus featured a broad green lawn in front, a basement that housed student lockers, and a separate gymnasium that stood between the two buildings.

"We thought it was a beautiful campus," remembered June Burtner, (Petaluma High Class of 1938.) "The lawns were well kept, and the buildings were nice."

Along with adjusting to his new academic environment, Gene also turned out for football, a passion he had developed as a youngster in grade school playing in the "big games" between the tiny towns of Cotati and Penngrove.

"I loved playing and wanted to play in high school," he said. "My brother Dan had played at Petaluma and was a real star. I was not nearly as big as he was. He was six-foot and about two hundred pounds. But I was much shorter and only about one hundred and fifty-five pounds."

"I never felt that I had to measure up to Dan, though," he went on. "Dan wasn't like that. He was a great guy and encouraged me to play up to my own abilities. So, I went out for the team and ended up playing center."

In the 1930's high school athletics were vastly different than today and football in particular defined that disparity. In lieu of the highflying aerial game that we know, most teams ran a variation of the single wing formation; a powerful ground attack that required split second timing, fundamental skills and a love for bone crushing contact. It was not a game for the faint of heart. Squads were small, substitutions were limited, and the boys played both offense and defense. The safety equipment of the day consisted of tiny leather shoulder pads that were so soft they resembled mushy pancakes, and offered about as much protection, and primitive leather helmets - "the kind you could fold up and put in your pocket," said one old player, with no facemasks. Smashed noses, cracked jaws and broken teeth were common. In a town like Petaluma, the rough and tumble brand of ball was a natural fit for the tough kids from the farms and ranches. Gene had no trouble fitting in with the other boys, many of whom were to become his life-long friends. One such boy was a fleet-footed athlete from Petaluma named Bob Acorne. Like Gene, Bob loved football and became a star for the Trojan eleven. Today, the retired business owner and salesman clearly recalls his days at Petaluma High.

"Gene and I played together all through high school," he said. "He played center and quarterback (blocking back) in the old single wing. He was smaller than his brother Dan but very tough and very good."

Gene had many friends like Bob and, by all accounts, the crowd he ran with, while not comprised of bad kids, was certainly not low key. As one can imagine, there were many incidents of mischief from such a band.

"My brother and I had learned to hunt when we were just kids," Gene remembered. "I'd take my single shot 410 and Dan would take his double barrel 12 gauge and we'd hunt pheasant, squirrels and just about everything on the ranch – anything that moved. My mother had a rule; 'Shoot to kill.' Shells were expensive and she didn't want us wasting them. We learned to be great shots because she expected us to hit what we aimed at. If it flew we shot it. We'd bring everything home and my mother would pick it or skin it and put it in the pot. Everyone hunted in those days."

"Well one day in my junior year, he continued, "I had my Dad's old Model A Ford. Normally I hitch-hiked to school after the morning chores were done. I had a deal with the principal,

Miss Ellen Trueblood, to skip first-period study hall. She knew I had to do the chores, and she let me arrive late. But on that morning I took a load of peas and potatoes to market. We always had the first crops of them in Northern California because we'd get no frost in the winter and we could get six or seven cents a pound for them. So anyway, I had the car that day and my pals and I decided to ditch school that afternoon and go hunting."

"So we piled in the Model A. I was driving, Bob Acorne was in the front, and Gene "Stiney" Stienbeck and Colin Holmes were in the back. We were driving down to San Antonio Creek, down along the Marin and Sonoma county line, and Colin started messing around with the gun in the back seat and the damn thing went off! I stopped the car to ask if anyone was hurt and no one was. I told Colin to stop playing with the damn gun. I was wearing a pair of cords, and looked down and saw that they were all bloody - I was hit in the leg! I was bleeding! Fortunately, the bullet had hit the doorpost before it hit my leg and so it wasn't so bad. Anyhow, we turned around and went back into town to Dr. Jim Anderson's office on 6th street to get me patched up."

What a scene it must have been, and indeed a scene that one would never see today. Petaluma's unholy four, ears pinned back like guilty dogs slithering into the doctor's office in the middle of a school day afternoon, two with concerned faces, one seeking medical attention and the other prowling the room seeking something else.

"The doctor looked at my leg," recalled Gene, "and told me he could patch it up. It burned like hell but all I wanted to know was if it would be OK for me to milk the cows that night. I also didn't want him to tell my mother. She would have been really upset if she knew I was not in school, not to mention the gun shot wound."

"So anyway," Gene laughed, "he told me that 'if you have to milk the cows, then milk the cows' and started sewing me up. At that point I noticed that his nurse was not there. She had been there when we came in but all of a sudden she was gone. As it turned out, she lived downstairs from Colin Holmes, and she and Colin had a "relationship". So while the doctor was patching me up and promising me that he wouldn't tell my mother, old Colin is in the other room getting a little of his "relationship" with the nurse!"

As Gene's high school career progressed and the depression ground on, the family's traditions and values continued to hold them together. "Our whole lives revolved around our home," said Gene. "My mother and father were so devoted to us. They supported us in everything we did. We felt comfortable there. They always encouraged us to bring our friends home, and we did."

"I spent a great deal of time up at the Benedetti house," remembered Bob Acorne. "They were great people and it was really a lot of fun. We used to call Gene's Dad "The Bosso." He was great. He'd always take us down to the wine cellar for a glass of wine."

"That was so funny," laughed Gene. "Dad always made a couple of hundred gallons of wine every year and maybe ten or twenty gallons of grappe (a distilled whiskey from wine). He totally ignored the law. In fact, I don't think he even knew there was a law. He'd make the wine in big fifty gallon barrels and then transfer it to smaller five gallon casks, each from a different year. He'd take the kids down there and start them off with a drink from a more recent vintage and before too long he'd 'graduate' them up to the older stuff with more alcohol in it. The guys would come stumbling out of that cellar … God it was funny. My mother would be so mad and Dad would light up with laughter."

"My parents just loved it," Gene went on. The guys always called my mom Pia. She loved to cook for them and it was a constant flow of kids, my brothers friends, my sisters friends and my friends in an out all the time."

Gene's parents did enjoy having a full house and Pia in particular took a special interest in her children's friends.

"My mother was not an educated woman but she was one of the most perceptive people I ever knew," Gene said. "She could size up a person with just a few questions and then tell you all about them. 'Be careful," she'd tell me about people, 'so and so won't stay with you if times are hard. Don't make an enemy – never do that – but he's not to be fully trusted.'"

One of Gene's best friends was a local boy named Gene "Stiney" Steinbeck. High spirited and creative, Stiney did not wear authority well and tended to channel his energy into various impieties that earned him a reputation – deserved or otherwise - as an incorrigible hell raiser.

"When we were in high school Stiney planted a smoke bomb under the hood of Miss Trueblood's car, laughed Gene. "We all stood up on the third floor of the school looking down as she and the Vice Principal got in and started the engine. The whole car started billowing with smoke. It was hilarious. You never saw two people vacate a car so fast. They called us all in, and the end result was that Stiney got kicked out of high school. He was always pulling something and most people thought he was a n'ere-do-well and would never amount to much. But my mom saw through all of that." 'He's a good person.' She told me. 'He'll stick by you, keep him as a friend.' "And she was right. Stiney is one of my best and loyal friends. She was never wrong – never."

The family also stuck together to make financial ends meet.

"By the time I was ready to finish high school I had spent every summer working with my brother and Dad," said Gene. "It was really tough. In the summers of my school years Dad took my brother Dan and I to work with him. We'd get up every morning and do the chores – that took about two hours – and then we'd all go to work together."

"There were two large seed farms in the valley, one called the Sherwood Farm and the other was called the Rohnert Farm. They were each about a mile long. All three of us worked those farms in the summer. We worked from sunup to after dark when they'd pull up pick-up trucks and turn on the lights so we could keep working. We'd dry the seeds on huge tarps and then Dan and I would feed them into the thrasher. It was always hot and dirty work and sometimes if we just couldn't keep going, we'd jam the thrasher so we could take a break. We got paid fourteen and one half cents per hour and, believe me, we were damn glad to get it! It was tough as hell, but a lot of people had it tougher. We never kept our money; we gave it all to my mother to pay the bills."

"You gain values when you live like that," he concluded. "You learn that family and the wisdom of your parents are valuable, and that keeping the family as the center of your life is all that is important."

****

In the fall of 1937 Gene was ready to enter his senior year of high school. It was to be his final year of Trojan football and as he and his teammates prepared for their season opener they looked forward to a successful campaign.

After two pre-season contests, a 13 – 6 win over the San Francisco City College Reserves - a tilt in which Gene's friend Bob Acorne scored on runs of twenty-five and fifty yards, and a 7-0 tune-up loss at the hands of San Francisco's Commerce High School reserve squad (a game in which the first team did not play) the Trojans were ready to launch their bid for a North Bay League title. Gene's teammates had voted him captain. The local newspaper, the *Argus Courier*, ran his picture on the day before the game. In the photo we see the fresh-faced farmer's son standing with his hands on his hips and smiling at the camera. Wearing his white practice uniform, his soft leather helmet is visible on the ground beside him and beneath his soiled jersey one can make out the outline of his tiny shoulder pads. His face reflects a curious mixture of innocence and experience, a boy about to take his final steps toward manhood.

The Trojans opened their 1937 North Bay League campaign against the Vallejo Apaches. The two teams were bitter rivals. In fact the year before, in a fight-marred contest played on the Petaluma grid, three players had been ejected. As a result, on Saturday, October 10, 1937, anxious athletic director J.C. Schuster, accompanied by a police escort, led an auto caravan of the Trojan faithful up the state highway to Vallejo's wet and muddy Corbus Field. Despite the enthusiastic fan support, along with the fine passing and brilliant receiving of Dave Livie and Bob Acorne respectively, the Trojans suffered a tough 7 – 6 loss. Accounts of the game did note, however, that the Petaluma line "Worked well…led by captain Gene Benedetti who played the entire game."

The following week the boys played host to the Napa Indians. Once again Acorne stood out with a seventy-five yard score. But the big break in the game came in the second quarter. With the contest still scoreless, and Napa driving for a touchdown, Gene intercepted a pass at midfield and sprinted toward the north goal. No one had ever accused Gene of being fast however, and his bid for glory was foiled when he was caught at the one-foot line. Fortunately, Butch Burtner came on and kicked a field goal to break the impasse as the Trojans went on to post a hard fought 15 – 0 victory. Another highlight that day was Trojan game announcer Curley Acorne (Bob's dad) who prowled the sidelines with a microphone and delivered a field-level play-by-play commentary to the fans.

1937 football season; "A mixture of innocence and experience..."

The Egg City Boys third league game was brutal as they traveled down to Marin County and took on the San Rafael Bulldogs. The match was rated a toss-up and fans were not disappointed. In a tough defensive struggle Bulldog running back Dick Schreiner outfoxed the Trojan defense when he scored from the five-yard line on a spectacular double reverse. It was all the boys from Marin needed as they handed the Trojans a heartbreaking 7 – 0 defeat.

The team had a bye the following week. However coach Paul "Pee Wee" Lathrop, frustrated with the poor play of his squad, demoted his entire first string, including Gene, telling local reporters that his seniors were becoming "overly satisfied" with themselves. To keep the team sharp, he arranged a scrimmage game with the Santa Rosa Junior College reserves, an uninspired outing that ended with neither team scoring.

Petaluma High School
class of 1939

The next Saturday brought Elmer Karlson's Analy High School Tigers to town. Unfortunately, the prior week's shake-up had done little to ignite the Trojan offense who continued their anemic ways playing the underdog Sebastopol club to scoreless tie.

Tamalipas High School was next up and the team finally came together. Bob Acorne, Russ Kynoch, Butch Burtner, Stiney Stienbeck, "Duke" Iverson and Gene Benedetti all played well in a 13 – 7 win over the Indians. The victory set up the Trojans "Big Game" with Santa Rosa High School. In anticipation the *Argus Courier* covered every day of practice in the tense week preceding the clash.

Saturday November 13, 1937 was the big day as Jimmy Underhill's Santa Rosa Panthers, sporting their vaunted Notre Dame offense, came to the wet and soggy fields of Petaluma to take on the Trojans. The two archrivals had played to a tie for two consecutive years and fans on both sides of the field hoped for a decisive break in the deadlock. The entire game, though hard-hitting and enthusiastic, was played in a blinding rainstorm that kept both squads from gaining an advantage in the thick black

1937 Petaluma Trojans. Gene is at center.

mud. Toward the end of the game, Santa Rosa's Eddie Dont completed a waterlogged pass to receiver Paul Mecchi. With the cold rain soaked fans on both sides screaming from beneath a rolling sea of black umbrellas, Mecchi sloshed twenty-eight yards down the sideline looking as if he would score to win the game. His bid for victory was thwarted, however, when Gene Benedetti and Bob Acorne combined to catch the speedy runner and drive him out of bounds on the eight-yard line. The tackle saved the day for the Trojans, and was a fitting end to the high school football career of the scrappy little center from Cotati.

ON TO COLLEGE

Santa Rosa J.C.; "Sturdy pivot man." 1938

VI

"If Shorty can get his paid for then he can go."

Pia Benedetti

On Thursday, June 8, 1938, Gene and the eighty-seven boys and one-hundred-thirteen girls of Petaluma High School's Class of 1938 walked in their graduation ceremony in the school gymnasium. It was an investiture into a unique club. Indeed in the America of the day, only one-half of the population went beyond eighth grade; only one in four finished high school and even less, one in five, held a college degree. For the vast majority of Americans like Gene, attending college in the still socially stratified nation was reserved for the moneyed elite. But five years earlier in 1933, Gene's older sister Milli had gone to St. Luke's School of Nursing in San Francisco. And two years later his older brother Dante had earned a football scholarship to Santa Clara University, where he stayed one year before transferring to the University of San Francisco. While Gene's sibling's academic pursuits were notable, they were not accomplished without conflict. In fact Giacondo had not wanted his children to attend college at all and his feelings caused quite a rift in the family. By today's standards, one in which a college education is common, his position seems unreasonable. But taken within the context of his culture, and the grim reality of the times, it made perfect sense.

Giacondo and Pia Benedetti were products of nineteenth century rural Italy. They were essentially farmers. Like most people of the soil they had little formal education. Giacondo had spent only two years in school, and Pia had barely gone beyond the third grade. For them, the measure of a person was taken in attributes like work ethic, faith, self-reliance and devotion to family. Out of necessity, they were a practical couple but they were not stodgy. In fact, Giacondo possessed a spirited joie de vivre and a sincere love for his wife and children. "He loved to be around people," said Gene. "His whole face would light up when he laughed, and he loved to drink wine and have a house full of friends."

Nonetheless, his views were driven by the practical realities of carving a living from his land. Thus the aesthetic limits of his thinking did not produce a connoisseur. "Why plant flowers?" he reasoned. "You can't eat them."

Years later Herm Benedetti remembered his grandfather like this: "He was definitely a no frills man," said Herm. "He never cared what things looked like. When he fixed a fence, he did it the old fashion Dago way; he patched it with anything he could find. It didn't get painted. It didn't matter what it looked like. As long as it kept the cows in, he didn't care."

For Giacondo the land and family represented all the wealth he could ever want or need. As long as his family was fed and healthy, he was content to work his land, play Bocci Ball on Sundays (an indulgence Pia allowed only if he went to church) and drink a little wine with his buddies. What else could there be?

Pia, on the other hand, was cut from a different cloth. A deeply religious woman, she viewed the world through a lens that recognized and appreciated God's handiwork. "I plant flowers because they are beautiful," she would say. While she was every bit as practical as her husband, she was also able to compare the opportunities in America with those in Italy. For her, America offered a chance for her children to reach beyond the fence line of a farmer's lot and achieve a life that would never have been possible in the old country. As a result, when Milli and Dante expressed a desire to go to college, Pia stood her ground and persuaded Giacondo to let them try. Money, of course, was an issue. In the 1930's the majority of working Americans earned less than $1,000 a year. Tuition at a school like the University of San Francisco was an astronomical $220 per year - far beyond the means of the Benedetti's. However, when as part of the nursing program, St. Luke's paid Milli's fees and Dante's superior athletic skills earned him a scholarship, the money issue was solved. With the precedent thus set, Gene was determined to follow in his sibling's footsteps.

"I wanted to go on to college and keep playing football," he said. "But I knew I had to get a football scholarship. There was just no way my parents could afford tuition. And I knew my grades weren't going to get me there. My dad was not for it but my mom told him, 'Milli and Dante went and it didn't cost us a dime. If Shorty can get his paid for, then he can go.'"

"My dad knew my mother." laughed Gene over half a century later. "There was no way he could talk her out of it. She was too tough. So I got to go as long as it was free."

There was also another problem. College football was and is a sport where size matters. This was especially true in the ground-oriented, grind-it-out style that dominated the game in the pre-war years. Indeed, a look at the 1940 USF roster reveals that out of twenty-three linemen, all but four were six feet or more in height and weighed at least two hundred pounds. Consequently, when compared to men like Doc Haley (6-3, 230lbs), Russ Kynoch (6.0 192lbs) Bill Telesmanic (6-3, 205lbs) and the massive Butch Burtner (6-4, 220lbs) Gene stood little chance of being recognized as a player who could compete at that level.

"I loved football," he said. "I knew from the very first that I wanted to play as long as I could and that I wanted to teach and coach football when I finished college. But there just wasn't room for a five foot nine inch one-hundred and seventy pound center."

But dreams die hard and Gene wasn't ready to let his go. Driven to acquire an education and to succeed in a game that he loved, he decided to give college a try at nearby Santa Rosa Junior College.

****

In 1907 California State Senator Anthony Caminetti of Amador County steered a bill through the California State Legislature that permitted high school boards of trustees to develop courses akin to those taught in the first two years of college. Caminetti's bill came as a result of the influence and support of two of California's most prominent educators, Dr. Alexis R. Lange, dean of the School of Education at the University of California, and Dr. David Starr Jordan, president of Stanford University. Lange and Jordan adhered to an educational theory developed by Dr. William Rainey Harper, the first president of the University of Chicago and the acknowledged "father of the junior college." Dr. Harper felt that the first two years of college were general (or junior) in nature and were but a prelude to the more important final two years that focused on specialization and research. Harper went on to suggest that these two "junior" years would be better spent at the local level. His views led to the establishment in 1901 of the nation's first junior college in Joliet, Illinois and in California, to the passage of Caminetti's bill. As a result, in 1910, public school officials in Fresno, California established the Golden States' first junior college. Similar institutions were soon opened in Hollywood in 1911 and Los Angeles in 1912. In 1918 the city of Santa Rosa followed suit and began to offer post high school graduate courses. Nine years later a junior college district was formed. Two years thereafter, in 1929, city fathers approved the building of a separate campus when they donated Burbank Park, a lovely 40-acre tract of land north of the downtown area. Construction began almost at once and in 1931 the school's first building, Pioneer Hall, was completed. Legend has it, that as a precondition to construction, no trees were to be removed from the land. Apocryphal or not, with its red brick buildings, bright colorful flower beds and lush green lawns shaded by ancient oak trees, the students and faculty of Santa Rosa JC can surely boast that of the more than 100 junior colleges in California, there are none that combine the grace and charm of nature more beautifully than theirs.

In the late 1930's, SRJC offered a wide range of classes and featured a fine athletic department. In addition to the major sports of football, basketball and baseball, men could participate in rugby, tumbling, and even ice hockey. The Women's Athletic Association offered badminton, horseback riding, volleyball, tennis, field hockey and basketball. The striking natural beauty of the school lent itself to a vibrant and active campus life. When the Bear Cubs played at home on Bailey Field, named for the schools first president Floyd P. Bailey, the stands were full of fans.

After his outstanding career at Petaluma High, football scouts in the area considered Gene an excellent acquisition. As a result, despite his diminutive size, coaches Dick Blewett and Cook Sypher were delighted to welcome him to the squad. As part of the Santa Rosa Unified School District the JC was not allowed to levy tuition and scholarships were not offered. But there were some concessions made for athletes. For example, Gene's primary mode of transportation was hitchhiking, a method much too unreliable for the commute from Cotati. Since the purchase of a car was out of the question, a need for housing arose. Coach Blewett stepped forward.

"The coaches arranged for some of us who didn't have a place to live to stay with football boosters," explained Gene. "I stayed with Judge Geary's brother Finlaw."

The son of a United States congressman, Superior Court Judge Donald Geary was a renowned jurist in northern California. Geary and his brother, well known attorney Finlaw, both generously supported the JC and loved Bear Cub football. Arrangements were made for Gene to stay with Finlaw and also to "help out" around the Geary family home on MacDonald Street in Santa Rosa. Built in 1895, the stately Victorian had originally been three stories until a fire partially burned it in the 1920's. Remodeled as a two story structure the mansion was an environment unlike any Gene had ever seen before.

"I had never been in a home like that and it was good for me," he said. "During the season, I'd stay up there during the week and hitchhike home on weekends to help with the chores. The Judge and Finlaw were great. I was appointed their official bartender. They'd have all kinds of prominent people over to the house and I'd pour their drinks. Finlaw was single and his parties were really something. The judge was married and a little more refined. But anyway, I got to meet all kinds of people. I met the Grace brothers who owned the local brewery and Red Tauzer who served on the board of trustees for the college. I'd never been around rich people like that and I learned that they were regular people - just like me."

With the housing problem resolved, Gene registered for classes and, along with his friend and teammate from Petaluma, Bob Acorne, turned out for the 1938 squad. The two former schoolboy stars quickly found that college ball was a different world. For one thing, the team was much larger. Indeed, with a nucleus of twelve returning veterans, combined with a full contingent of newcomers, coach Blewett found himself blessed with a team that was three deep at virtually all positions. The players were also bigger, especially the linemen. But, as always, Gene found a way. Endowed with excellent balance, sound fundamentals and a fearless toughness, he soon made his presence known and found himself in the thick of the action.

Coach Blewett's platoon system showed its effectiveness early when in the season's first two practice games the Bear Cubs hammered the San Francisco Boys Club 45-0 and beat the College of the Pacific Frosh by a score of 19-6. Gene played well enough in his first two college games to rate a picture and article in the local *Press Democrat* that referred to him as the "sturdy pivot man" in the Bear Cub offense. The article went on to predict that the freshman would see plenty of action in the upcoming Bear Cubs final practice game (a 26-0 thumping of the California Aggies).

On the Saturday after beating the Aggies, the Cubs traveled to Auburn and opened conference play against Placer Junior College. The game was played in a steady downpour causing observers to remark that the Bear Cub band blew more bubbles than music. In spite of the sodden conditions, the Cubs put their first conference win under their belt, whipping the Miners by a score of 12-0. Blewett's Boys returned home the following week to face the University of California Ramblers in a mid-season practice game. Over 4,000 faithful fans jammed into Bailey Field for the contest only to see the heavier and more experienced Ramblers hand their boys a tough 25-15 defeat.

But the loss paid dividends on the following Saturday night. With more than half the Santa Rosa student body cheering in the stands the hardened Cubs traveled down to Kentfield and pounded out a soggy 12-0 win over the Marin JC Mariners.

The boys from Burbank Park, now poised to make a run at the conference title, were not to be denied. Taking on a bigger Menlo College club they employed a high-flying aerial attack and handed the Oaks a 19-0 defeat. The next week, in the conference final, Salinas College gave the Cubs a scare when they scored first to go in front 7-0. But, ignited by an electrifying sixty-five yard sweep around the end by Bob Acrone, the Blue and Red stormed back, scoring once in the air and twice on smashing runs off tackle. By the time the final gun popped over the cheers of the sell out crowd, the Bear Cubs had posted a 19-7 win over the Panthers and taken the conference championship. It was the first title in the school's twenty-one year history. When Gene and Bob were voted onto the all-conference team it was a well-deserved icing on the championship cake for the two country kids from Petaluma.

Along with the championship and platitudes, Gene also garnered notice from schools other that Santa Rosa. "After that first season, my buddy from high school, Duke Iverson and I were contacted by the University of Oregon," Gene remembered.

"Duke was a year behind me and was a great player – the best we had – and Oregon wanted he and I to come up and play ball." The school went so far as to send the boys bus fare and invited the pair up for a campus visit.

"Gene got the idea that we should keep the money," recalled Iverson. "He told me we could keep it and hop a freight train up to Oregon."

"God what a time," he went on. "We hitched up to Davis to catch the train going north to Oregon. The train came through about 6:30 in the morning. We thought it would just be poking along but instead this big monster came rumbling through at bout 60 miles an hour! There was no way we could hop it. We had to hitch hike. We got as far as Redding and we stayed in an old beat-up hotel. The next morning we went out to the end of Redding and started hitching for a ride. A car came by and dropped a young lady off. She wanted to hitchhike with us. She wasn't there two minutes and some guy stopped and picked her up but left us there. We stayed in Redding and then got a Dollar Line bus for a dollar up to Grants Pass, Oregon. We got out and started hitch hiking again. Pretty soon, along came this same gal with the guy who had picked her up. We were standing out in the cold and they waved to us as they drove by. Finally the police came along and booted us out of town – they didn't like transit traffic I guess."

After several hours of getting nowhere hitching in the freezing night the ever-resourceful Gene had another idea. "I figured if we stayed out in the cold we'd freeze," he said. "So we went back into town to the jail. I told the jail keep that since, after all we were vagrants, that maybe he could let us sleep in the jail. The guy laughed and said sure, so we got to sleep in the nice warm cell for the night. Not a bad deal!"

At last the two wayward footballers-vagrant-jailbirds, arrived in Eugene. "The coaches worked us out to see what we could do," recalled Gene, "and then told us they wanted us to come up and play ball for them."

"At first I was really excited, but then I talked to my brother Dan. He was a senior at USF and had enjoyed a great career. He sat me down and asked me where I wanted to live after college. When I told him Cotati, he advised me to go to school somewhere in the bay area if I planned on living in northern California. I decided to follow his advice, so Duke went on to Oregon and I stayed home for another year at the JC. But hell, it was a great adventure!"

****

With Gene's adventures as a hobo, and Dante's graduation from USF, the spring of 1939 was not only a busy time for the family but also proved to be a joyous one with the marriage of their daughter Emily.

In an era in which women were expected to assume the role of a housewife and mother, Emily "Milli" Benedetti stood apart. After graduating from high school - with her mother's encouragement and her fathers grudging acceptance – she had stepped beyond the social mores of the day and moved to San Francisco where she enrolled at St. Luke's School of Nursing. Located at the corner of Valencia and Army streets, St. Luke's operated under the auspices of the Episcopalian Church and was a typical nursing school of the times. In lieu of tuition, students in the three-year program worked in the hospital as part of their study. It was hands-on nursing from the bottom up and trainees learned early if they had what it took. Apparently Milli did, for three years after she enrolled in the program she donned the starched "whites" of a Registered Nurse and proudly graduated from the four-story yellow brick hospital in The City's Mission District. Upon her return home she joined the ranks of the relatively small number of working women in America, taking a job as a surgical nurse at the Sonoma County Hospital. Bright and beautiful, she was articulate, straightforward and independent. By all accounts, Milli Benedetti was quite a catch.

Lucien G. "Red" Libarle was seven years Milli's senior when his sister Irene arranged for the two to meet on a blind date. The son of French immigrants, Red had also been raised in a family where hard work was a fact of life.

In March of 1915 Red's French speaking parents, Jean and Laurence had established the Lace House French Laundry at 128 Liberty Street in Petaluma.

"In an era before synthetic fibers and washing machines, running a laundry was a difficult and demanding business", said Red's son, Dan Libarle, who operates the business today.

"Every day my grandfather would send a horse-drawn wagon around town and out to the Russian River to pick up dirty clothes and linens. All of the rich people sent in their stuff. We did everything; clothes, undergarments, women's foundations, table linens, everything."

The laundry also catered to many commercial accounts. "In those days," Libarle explained, "travel was much more time consuming and people who came to town stayed overnight. Businesses like the Hotel Petaluma and the Yosemite Hotel, as well as hotels out on the river all had dining rooms that used linen tablecloths and napkins. That, along with their bed clothes generated a lot of business."

"It was a tough business," Dan continued. "My grandfather did all of the washing by hand on a washboard and grandmother Laurence, did all of the pressing. She'd heat the irons on a perforated grill over a fire. It was all done by feel. She knew how hot each iron was and never scorched the fabric. In the summer with no air conditioning … it was brutal."

Grandmother Laurence also cooked for the French-speaking employees who worked in exchange for room and board. "They all worked together and lived on the second floor above the laundry," Dan said. "My dad grew up that way. He learned the business from the ground up. He started as a little boy riding the wagon and helping load the laundry bags. Dad came up tough."

Along with being assiduous, the Libarle household was also deeply religious. By the time he was introduced to Milli, Red was seriously considering entering the priesthood.

"Red was handsome, and I really liked him," Milli laughed years later. "So did my brothers, even though they teased me and said he was 'kind of puny'."

The couple dated for a while until Milli, in typical Benedetti fashion, called the meeting to order. "You can't be a priest and marry me," she told Red. "What do you want to do?"

Red Libarle was nobody's fool. Milli was beautiful and he was in love. And so, on April 25, 1939, both families gathered under the Spanish tiled spires of St. Vincent's Church in Petaluma to witness Reverend James Kiely celebrate the wedding mass that united the couple in a marriage that was to last until Red's death over fifty-six years later.

****

With Milli married and Dante off to Los Angeles to attend graduate school, Gene set about preparing for his second year of college. Like most young Americans that summer he had little awareness and less concern of world events. In the 1930's there was no TV, never mind cable to transmit news. And radio broadcasts, such as they were, were seldom heard in real time. These factors, coupled with the fact that most people were trying to cast off the shackles of the depression, made a conflict in Europe seem as distant as a sand storm on the moon. Buttressed by friendly neighbors and insulated by two vast oceans, Americans felt safe and disconnected from events so far away. Accordingly, when German panzers rumbled across the flat Polish countryside in the pre-dawn darkness of September 1, 1939, to start World War Two, Gene took little notice. He was far more focused on keeping his grades up, repeating his all conference performance, and attracting enough attention to earn a scholarship.

"I had no idea about what was going on overseas," said Gene. "It had no affect on our lives. To us it was a long way off and best solved by someone else."

Thus with global events as an unnoticed backdrop, Gene returned to Santa Rosa for a final year at the JC. By this time he had many friends on campus and instead of returning to the Geary's, took up residence in an off campus house with some of the football players. "It was a little less restrictive," he chuckled.

His second season at the JC was a repeat of the first as coach Blewett once again fielded a powerful team that quickly dispatched their first three pre-season opponents beating Stockton J.C. the Cal Aggie Frosh and the San Jose State Babes respectively. On

October 13, the Bear Cubs opened conference play when they hosted Placer J.C. at Bailey Field. This time, however, the Miners were inspired and managed to hand the injury riddled Cubs a tough 6-0 defeat. It was to be the Cubs only loss of the season. The following week, with their injuries healed, the Blue and Red stormed back to thrash Yuba J.C. 36-0 before traveling to Salinas where they played to a 0-0 tie in the Lettuce Bowl, a game played in a fog so dense " ... you couldn't see across the line of scrimmage." The country clubbers from Menlo were next up for Blewett's Boys who, using a trademark aerial attack leavened with several fine runs, defeated the Oaks 13-6. The following week the Bear Cubs "Big Game" with "Scoop" Carlson's Marin Mariners turned into a rout as the Blue and Red ripped off a 36-0 victory. Just like that, Santa Rosa had won their second consecutive championship. The team played a farewell game on November 18, traveling to Reno to finish the season with a 7-0 victory over the University of Nevada Frosh. The final win and the championship was a fine finish to a two-year career that not only saw Gene earn another spot on the all conference squad, but also helped to make history for the beautiful little college in Burbank Park.

After his stellar career in junior college Gene found himself a hot property as college recruiters came calling for his services.

"I had offers from Oregon, Nevada and even Stanford," he recalled. "I thought I might go to Stanford but my grades were not high enough." But when he was offered a scholarship from the University of San Francisco, it wasn't much of a decision. Gene would follow his brother to The City to play for the Dons. For the tough little lineman from Cotati – the kid who was too small for college ball - it was a portentous sign that the best was yet to come.

CUS

Program cover from the 1940 Sun Bowl in El Paso, Texas.

VII

***"The boys were very close.
Rock wouldn't leave home without Cus."***

Ida Pirro

On New Years' day 1940 a crowd of 13,000 football fans filed into El Paso's Kidd Field on the campus of the Texas College of Mines and Metallurgy (present day University of Texas El Paso) to watch the Bulldogs from Tempe Normal Teachers College (now Arizona State University) play the top ranked Flying Cardinals from Catholic University in the fifth annual Sun Bowl. The game between the private Catholic school from urban Washington DC and the public teachers college from the sun-baked deserts of the west was the grand finale of El Paso's annual Sun Carnival. Sponsored by local service clubs, the theme for the carnival that year was "America". The weeklong fiesta with its concerts, horse shows, dances and the Pageant of America Parade was the highlight of the year in the dusty border city on the Rio Grande. The event not only captured the attention of local citizens but also drew thousands of El Paso's Mexican neighbors to the gala attractions and grand parade on New Years' day.

For Catholic University's Carmon "Cus" Pirro and his older brother Rocco, the festive carnival and the game in the sun-splashed stadium was a fitting finish to a career that had started four years earlier in their hometown of Solvay, New York.

Cus and Rocco – who everyone called Rock - were two of eight children born to Thomas and Marian Pirro. Reared in the depression, the brothers had grown up helping their father in his job as a milkman for the Silverbrook Dairy.

"Thomas was a fine man," recalled Rocco's wife Ida. "He delivered milk to the entire village. During the Depression, when families ran short of money, he'd carry them on credit until they could pay. He saw to it that no family in Solvay went without milk."

Cus Pirro; rugged tackle for the flying Cardinal's of Catholic University, circa 1940. Courtesy Catholic University.

The Pirro's was a warm and traditional Italian home, one in which Marian opened her kitchen to everybody, making every visitor feel comfortable and accepted. As a result the two brothers were extremely close to their family and to each other. When they approached high school graduation, Thomas offered to buy the dairy so they could all work together. But the brothers were also great athletes and in 1935, when the burly six-foot 220lb Rocco graduated from Solvay High School, college recruiters came calling. But Rock was reluctant to leave without his younger brother.

Rocco Pirro as a Flying Cardinal in 1940.
Courtesy Ida Pirro.

"They were very close," remembered Ida. "Rock didn't want to be alone at school so he took postgraduate classes for a year and waited for Cus. When Cus graduated the following spring, Catholic University offered both of the boys a scholarship."

Rock with the Pittsburgh Steelers 1941.
Courtesy Ida Pirro.

The Pirro brother's arrival at CU as a package proved to be a wise investment for the school as the pair played both football and basketball. In their senior year, the tough running (and team captain) Rock won the scoring title of the District of Columbia when he amassed 36 points. While Cus, the hard hitting lineman, was not only the teams leading tackler, but also ranked with the top place kickers in the country, converting 18 out of 21 points after touchdown.

The Pirro's as a package was a wise investment of the Cardinals. Courtesy Ida Pirro.

When they led the 8-1 Flying Cardinals onto the floor of the Sun Bowl that bright Texas afternoon, it was the final chapter in a defining experience that had shaped their individual futures. Rock, the tough and talented fullback, who upon his graduation would be a twelfth-round draft choice of the Pittsburgh Steelers, was destined for the spartan world of professional football. Cus, on the other hand, had chosen a more intellectual pursuit.

"Cus was the scholar of the two," said Ida. "When he finished college he applied and was accepted to Catholic University's law school."

The Pirro Brothers were very close. "Rock waited a year for Cus so he would not have to go off to school alone." Courtesy Catholic University.

After the game, a tough defensive battle that ended in a scoreless tie, the two teams boarded trains bound for their respective homes. As the eastbound steamer rumbled across the trackless landscape Cus sat with his older brother and watched the black night pass beyond the window. He had no way of knowing that events a world away had linked his future to Gene Benedetti's and that their paths were destined to cross in the deadly drama of a terrible war.

USF

St. Ignatius Church on the USF campus, circa 1940

VIII

"A Jesuit college for the youth of the city . . ."

Father Anthony Maraschi S.J.

Founder of USF 1855

As the winter of 1940 stretched into spring the war in Europe was heating up. After defeating Poland, Hitler had turned on the rest of the continent. In April Denmark and Norway fell. In May his Blitzkrieg stunned the world when it turned on France and overran the entire country – a debacle that climaxed with the English Expeditionary Force (sent to help the embattled French) being pushed into the sea at Dunkirk where they were gallantly rescued by British citizens in a ragtag fleet of fishing boats, yachts, and dories.

The conquest of France culminated on June 14, 1940 when, in the same railroad car that German generals had capitulated in twenty-two years earlier, the beleaguered French bowed to the Nazi's in a humiliating ceremony of surrender.

Gene's response to all of this was typical of most Americans.

"I hardly knew it was happening," he recalled. "My mind was on starting school at USF."

Standing like a spire bedecked diva atop the Ignatian Heights; the University of San Francisco is a testament to Catholic tradition and Jesuit faith. Indeed, even the university's first president and founder, Father Anthony Maraschi S.J., could hardly have imagined the circuitous journey the school would take before finding its present home on the fifty-one acre campus at Fulton and Parker streets.

Founded in 1855 in a simple wooden church on Market Street, the College of St. Ignatius served the spiritual and educational needs of the surrounding community for twenty-five years. By the late nineteenth century, as San Francisco began to develop as a major city and cultural center, city fathers envisioned a grand

The Brawl, circa 1940

boulevard to rival the Champs de Elyesse of Paris. The result was Van Ness Avenue, a wide promenade lined with stately homes and buildings where, in 1880, the benefactors of St. Ignatius built a splendid new college and church. But in April of 1906, when the great San Francisco earthquake and fire leveled The City, the beautiful buildings along Van Ness either burned or were dynamited to create a firebreak. When the vast clouds of smoke finally cleared, all that remained of St. Ignatius was a pile of smoking rubble and the stubborn resolve of her Jesuit fathers.

Hence in 1910, after a temporary stay at Hayes and Shrader Streets, ground was broken for a new church on the hilltop at Fulton and Parker Streets. Engineer John E. Pope, envisioned the church as a building with "towering outlines visible from all parts of the City ... with stately towers piercing the air above the breakers."

It was also to be a building that would survive another earthquake and last forever. Toward that end he and architect J.I. Devlin designed an edifice that was framed in steel. When it was finally dedicated in 1914, the beautiful "Jesuit Baroque" church with its majestic twin spires and massive columns rising 200 feet above the street was an immutable tribute to the conviction, vision, and skill of its builders.

In the fall of 1940, when Gene Benedetti arrived, the campus was a much different institution than the coeducational, multicultural university of today. Typical of the approximately twenty-five Jesuit colleges in America at the time, USF was all male, small (less than 1,000 students), relatively expensive, and rigidly structured. Basic tuition was $75 per semester. Incidental costs included $10 for lab fees, $3 for registration, $5 for student government tax, a student health fee of $1.50 and library charges of $2.50. Books totaled about $15.00 and seniors were really hit when they were assessed an additional $13.50 as a graduation fee.

In addition to the costs, the curriculum was prearranged and exacting. A look at the 1940 catalog revels that, except for freshmen, who were limited to 16 units, candidates for a degree were required to take 18 units per semester and comply with the following:

1. Complete 128 units or semester hours of work in prescribed and elective courses leading to the degree desired.

2. Maintain an average grade of at least C for the entire course.

3. Complete a written thesis of not less than 5,000 words on a subject chosen from the student's major field with the approval of the Chairman of the Department.

4. Attain an average of C in his major.

5. Take a comprehensive examination in his major field at the end of Senior Year with at least a grade of C.

6. Spend at least the last year of his course in residence at the university taking at least a minimum schedule.

7. Merit at least a passing grade in any oral examinations prescribed by the Committee on Scholarship.

The Society of Jesus (the Jesuits), an order founded by Saint Ignatius Loyola (1491-1556), ran the university and it's instructor-priests were considered to be among the most scholarly of the clergy.

"The road to ordination for a Jesuit took about thirteen years," explained University Archivist Fr. Michael Kotlanger S.J. "It included training in religious life, instruction in prayer and spirituality, language classes, physical labor in the agricultural fields and four to six years of university work leading to a degree in one of the scholarly disciplines. After acquiring his degree, the seminarian was sent to a Jesuit high school to teach or coach for a few years after which he would return to school to earn a graduate degree in Theology."

"By the time he arrived at a school like USF," Kotlanger concluded, "he was well trained and ready."

A panel of upperclassmen called the Board of Student Control directed the social and behavioral standards on campus, seeing that students maintained a demeanor consistent with "Gentlemanly deportment ... toward officials, instructors, and other members of the University ... " and – at risk of the "severest possible penalties" – did not gamble, drink or possess intoxicants.

Moreover, lest he be accused of "inappropriate vesture unbecoming a gentleman", USF men were required to wear a collared shirt, long pants with a belt (no jeans permitted), a jacket or sweater and shined leather shoes.

Proper respect and manners were a matter of course. Whenever the President or Dean of the College entered a room the students were to rise until the esteemed leader had been seated. Each day at noon, and again at 6pm the bell in the campanile tolled and students, faculty and staff who were outdoors, would stop and silently say a prayer (the Angelus) which recalled the scripture story of the angel Gabriel announcing to Mary that she was to become the mother of Jesus the Son of God. Indeed, USF and higher education in general was a much different world in 1940 than it is today.

"It was very disciplined," Gene said. "There was no horsing around. The priests were very scholarly and kept you on track and you really had to put out. We sat for exams – sometimes oral exams – and you really had to be ready."

"But," he went on, "it was fun. We always knew where we stood. And I think that sometimes the priests gave us a break. We were athletes and most of them had more than a little sports fan in them. Football brought a lot of attention to the school. And while I can't prove it, I always felt that they gave us a break once in a while."

Along with affording the boys some latitude, the priests also offered guidance and assistance and at least two Jesuits played a role in Gene's development during his years at USF.

Fr. Hubert Flynn, S.J. was a long time Dean of Liberal Arts and Science. Kind, well spoken and scholarly, Father Flynn taught philosophy before and after his deanship. But older alumni, especially the student-athletes, remember him as a wise and trusted counselor.

"He was a great guy," recalled Gene's classmate, Jim Grealish. "He kept so many of us in school. One of our classmates, Pete Breceda, was from Santa Monica. Pete used to leave on Thursday and go home. He'd come back on the following Tuesday. We called it taking a 'Santa Monica Weekend'. When too many guys were doing stuff like that Father Hub would have a talk with them to set them straight. If someone was having trouble with a class, he would go to the teacher, find out the problem and then have a talk with the student. He'd do anything he could to keep a guy in school." Gene confirmed: "He was no nonsense and tough. He was a little guy but he'd stand right up to you. He did it the right way though, he'd just talk to you quietly and let you know he cared about you and your progress. But, he never hesitated to correct any of us who were getting out of line - and there was plenty of that I can tell you. We all respected him. We called him Father Flynn to his face, but in our hearts he was always, "Father Hub."

Today the Annual Alumni Athletic Hall of Fame Dinner is named in his honor. And although he has been deceased for nearly sixty years the good "Father Hub" remains a respected and beloved figure in the traditions of the university, and in the memories of those who knew him.

As a student-athlete, Gene was not only exempt from tuition and fees, but was also provided with an on-campus job.

"Oh sure, we had jobs" he laughed. "We didn't work too hard, though. I had it made. I got to work for Father Rossi."

Related to the founders of the famous Italian Swiss Colony Winery in Asti, California the tres elegant Rev. Carlo P. Rossi, S.J. came to USF in 1940. In the 1920's he had been a salesman for the Stauffer Chemical Corporation before trading in his business suit and briefcase for the vestments of a Jesuit. A profound scholar and language specialist, Rossi was also the director of buildings and grounds and ran campus work projects.

"He was the official gardener," laughed Gene. "He kept the beautiful flowers around the buildings and spoke classic Italian. 'Geno,' he'd say, 'veine lavorar con me' (come work with me). I was a farmer's son. I loved to work in the garden. Hell, I felt guilty taking the money. But we'd work together and converse in Italian. I loved it. Father Rossi was really a great man."

"You have to understand," he went on, "It was like a family. The school was so small and we saw each other every day. It was not at all like it is today."

Indeed, it was not; in contrast to today, with its over fifty acres of modern buildings, dormitories, and athletic fields, the university in 1940 consisted of two buildings and a church.

Almost all campus life revolved around one building, Campion Hall. Built in 1927, the three story structure housed the Law School and library on the top floor while the rest of the building held all of the administration offices and classrooms for the college as well as the student lounge (complete with a small snack bar) in the basement. Between The Hall and the church stood a smaller building that served as a residence hall for the priests. The entire athletic department consisted of a practice field for the football team and a small shack for the coach's offices.

Despite its size and regulations the campus was active and exciting. For example, during the second week of the fall semester each year an annual contest called The Brawl was held between the freshman and sophomore classes. Events included jousts, tie-up, sack races, relay races, and the Ball Rush, a rowdy event in where a mob from each class sought to push a gigantic ball over their opponents' goal. The Brawl culminated with the quest for "The Cap" an event where men from each side tried to shinny up a greased poll and snatch a school cap off the top. On the Saturday after The Brawl the sophomore class hosted a dance honoring the new freshmen. At Christmas, in the glittering splendor of hotels like the Palace or the Mark Hopkins, the Associated Students sponsored a dance for the men and their dates. Activities sponsored by the speech and debate societies, as well as those of the student band, symphony orchestra and glee club were also part of the campus scene. Each spring, the school play, a major event directed by James Gill - a talented and respected lay professor for whom today's campus theatre is named - entertained the students. Two student publications, the *San Francisco Foghorn* and the *San Francisco Literary Quarterly*, as well as the local commercial press, reported on these activities.

"I loved it," recalled Gene. "There was always something going on. We all knew each other, and there was a lot of support and participation."

USF was a streetcar college. The student body was primarily comprised of local boys who lived at home and commuted to class via public transportation. Since there were no dormitories on campus, out of town athletes like Gene were billeted in houses that were rented or leased by the university.

"It was called the Varsity House," chuckled Gene. "The locations changed each year depending on what was available. Because my brother Dan had brought his friends to visit us in Cotati, I knew many of the guys already. It made it a lot easier for me. Doc Haley, Joe Clerou, Tom Rice, Bebe Moore, Tiger Smith, Bill Telesmanic, and Blaze Miatovich - I knew them all from Dan. Plus Butch Burtner and Russ Kynoch from Petaluma High were there so I had some guys from home."

As one would expect, a group of high-spirited young men living together in a house produced more than a few rowdy stories.

"My brother Dan had lived with a bunch of guys in a three story Victorian in the 1800 block of Turk street," laughed Gene. "He and Tom Rice were in charge of the house. That was like hiring a bank robber as police chief. I used to visit him and watch him and his pals grease the streetcar tracks in front of the house. The streetcars would come along and spin their wheels and try to make the hill. They never made it. We'd sit on the front porch and drink beer and laugh. We never got caught."

"We had a similar atmosphere," he went on. "It was one thing after another. In my senior year Mal McCarthy and I bought a car. That was really something. It was a four door touring car – a Dodge I think – and it was really plush. It was a beautiful light tan and had running boards and a spare tire on each side – it was really something to see. Some old man out in the avenues had it up on blocks in his garage and sold it to us for $150.00. Boy, were we living!"

"That car was really something," confirmed Jim Grealish. "Most of the guys that bought cars got them from Buolitti's used lot on Geary Street. You could go in there and buy a "second hand second hand" clunker for $10.00. But Benedetti and McCarthy's car – that was the leader of the pack!"

But the campus activities, cruising with the guys, and spirited camaraderie of the Varsity House notwithstanding, the greatest attraction for the boys was the incomparable City of San Francisco.

The irrepressible Mal McCarthy behind the wheel of "The Car."

CITY LIFE

America's Tiffany Diamond, circa 1940

IX

"... It's the indescribable conglomeration of beauty and ugliness that makes San Francisco a poem without meter, a symphony without harmony, a painting without reason – a city without an equal."

San Francisco Columnist Herb Caen, 1940

If Chicago was Carl Sandburg's City of Broad Shoulders, San Francisco in the fall of 1940 was America's Tiffany Diamond. From the gilded mansions of the great railroad barons on Pacific Heights, to the churning alleys of China Town - where the sounds and smells of the mysterious East rolled down Grant Avenue and spilled into the Italian streets of North Beach, The City thrived like a living being. Along the foggy waterfront white capped Stevedores shouted through the mist as they loaded and unloaded exotic cargos from all corners of the globe. Just up the hill, the smell of Ghirardelli chocolate mixed with the burning scent of pinewood brakes as drivers clanged their bells and squeezed their cable cars to stop outside the Buena Vista Café. And of course there was the beautiful bay; dotted with lovely green islands and sporting two new bridges - one a looming link to the plebian city of Oakland, and the other a golden portal to the open sea. Where on a sunny day the wakes of ferryboats, barges and ocean liners painted feathered white brush strokes on a sparkling blue canvas of water.

San Francisco was a city that changed from metropolis one moment to small town the next. A place where elegant women dressed in heels and gloves shopped in grand department stores like The City of Paris and Gumps - with its cachet of priceless objects d'art - and then walked a few blocks to China Town to eat lunch in the back streets of a mandarin village. From the top of the thirty-two-story Russ Building (built in 1927), one could see the clock on the Ferry Building at the foot of Market Street, where the tang of salty air off the bay mixed with the heady aroma of roast coffee from the Folgers and Hills Brothers coffee plants. A German lunch at Schroeder's on Market – men only please and sit where we tell you – cost $.85, and a great dinner – select from the menu on the blackboard - was a $1.15 – ladies with escorts tolerated.

For a boy like Gene, whose veins flowed with the blood of the land, San Francisco swept over the senses unlike anything else in the world.

"I had never seen anything like it," he remembered fondly. "I had been to The City a few times to visit, but now I was living there and it was magnificent."

But in truth, Gene was still a rube from the country and roaming The City whose streets resonated with the sounds and smells of far away places was a fantastic practical education.

Joe Clerou, a teammate of both Gene and his brother Dan, was from Bakersfield, California, a small farming and oil town that one day would produce Buck Owens and "The Buckaroos". A country boy at heart, Joe had come to The City one year earlier and compared to Gene, was an urban sophisticate.

"I kind of took Gene under my wing," he laughed over sixty years later. "He was so gullible it wasn't funny. He had no idea of what to do or how to act. One time we were walking down Haight Street - this was before it went hippie - and some guy was selling an electric shaver. An electric shaver was really a novel item at the time and Gene just had to have it. It never occurred to him that it might be stolen merchandise."

"So anyway," he went on, "Gene talked the guy down from five bucks to three and thought he'd really gotten a deal."

Apparently the new accessory was not as efficient as promised.

"The damn thing wouldn't cut at all," laughed Clerou. "It tore the whiskers out of his face one by one. I called it the 'go get em' razor because it just went and grabbed the whiskers and ripped em' out by the roots. God you should have seen his face! He ended up trading it to Pete Breceda for a yellow rain coat."

But rube or not, Gene was now a university man and, with many of his social contacts already established, fit easily into the academic (and sometimes rowdy) bonhomie of college life. As part of his education away from the shadow of the Jesuits, he and his friends often took field trips to The City's more historic sites - some of which were notable enough to warrant a return visit or two. One such excursion led through the portals of a dingy little tavern at 45 Eddy Street and into the world of the immortal Shanty Malone.

Born in 1897, Aloysius Patrick "Shanty" Malone was one of the great treasures of a San Francisco long past. By the time he died in 1982, he had operated a series of drinking and bookmaking establishments in nine different locations for as long as anyone could remember. A man of no pretensions, Shanty dressed like an unmade bed, kept the messiest tavern in town and was judged by those for whom he poured a thousand drinks as the finest saloonkeeper in The City. Malone's taste for interior design catered to those of his customers, an eclectic jockaucracy that happily drank sitting under the inverted goal posts that hung from the dank ceiling and loved to play football on a grimy floor painted with yard markers.

When things got dull – which wasn't often - Shanty would hold a cockfight. On at least one occasion during the prohibition years, he staged a phony raid, hustling his patrons out the back door, only to welcome them back through the front a few minutes later.

Shanty's emporium welcomed all species: from the guy who dove head first into the floor for a beer – and thereby kept alive the tradition of the famed Oftie Goofty, a local nut from years past who scrounged free drinks by allowing himself to be hit with a baseball bat - to the drunken professional wrestler who choked out patrons after a few too many, and of course to the "goat man" who, after draining his glass, ate it.

At Shanty's, the lads from USF felt right at home. As one can imagine, the stories emanating from such a place are legend. Once such tale is still repeated among old time USF'ers and since no account of Shanty's is complete without it we retell it here for posterity. As the story goes, Doc Haley and Tom Rice along with a few of the boys (it has never been established just who "the boys" were) spent a weekend at the Benedetti's in Cotati. Warmed by the abundance of Pia's cooking and hospitality, not to mention a trip or two to The Bosso's wine cellar, the good lads found themselves making an arduous and blurry return to The City on Sunday night. But before returning to the care of the Jesuits, they felt the need for a final libation. Showing a natural gift for leadership, Doc Haley took charge and drove to Shanty's, where the boys fell out of the car and stumbled in for a final toast.

Surprisingly – or maybe not - a final drink turned into an extended drunk. Finally good sense prevailed and the besotted coterie of Dons rose from their bar stools, piled into the car and took off. They had gone no more than twenty yards, however when, to their complete surprise, they found themselves up on the sidewalk, a string of scattered garbage cans in their wake. At this point, fearing a blot on the schools escutcheon, Doc Haley once again stepped forward. Clearing his throat the future attorney and legal scholar turned to the massive Tom Rice; "Tom," he intoned, "you've been drinking, I think I'd better drive."

The huge red head and one day professional wrestler struggled to focus his eyes as he slowly lifted his head. "But Doc," he replied thickly, "you are driving!"

"I wasn't there, I swear it" laughed Gene, throwing up his hands in mock horror. "But oh my, what a place Shanty's was. We went in there day or night. He kept it open 24 hours a day. Hell, all of the cops were his friends – either that or he paid them off. God what a place!"

"San Francisco was so rich in culture and so available," he went on. "You could take a date dancing at the Palace Hotel, listen to one of the world's great dance bands and then go catch Rusty Draper sing in the Rumpus Room at Will Kings Koffee Kup at 18th and Geary and not spend five dollars for the entire evening!"

Along with the social and academic life in The City, Gene continued to return home on weekends whenever he could. "My friends and I used to head up to Cotati on weekends," he recalled. "My mom and dad loved it. If more than expected showed up, Mom would just go out back and kill another chicken. She'd cook a big dinner and Dad would take the boys down to the cellar and get them drunk. It was so much fun. I'd bring the whole team home, and we'd have a great time. When it was in season we'd lift a gallon of Dad's wine and go to the Russian River."

"Oh heavens yes," laughed Milli. "The river was really the place. We had been going there for years. Both Shorty and Dan would bring their friends home and we'd all head to the river to go dancing."

"All the big bands came to the river," said Gene. "We saw them all. The two towns, Gurennville, and Rio Nido had dance clubs – a place called The Grove was a big one - but they had a cover charge. We never had much money so we'd send one guy in to get his hand stamped and then one of my friends would take a pen and copy the stamp on our hands so we could get in for free. It was great. We were athletes and people knew us so inevitability someone would buy us a drink. Anson Weeks was one of the big bands in those days. I'll never forget him."

Oakland born Anson Weeks, known as, "The King of Nob Hill", led the house band at the elegant Mark Hopkins Hotel. Weeks' music, considered some of the most danceable ever played, was broadcast coast to coast each week on his "Lucky Strike Magic Carpet" radio program. In the tourist season, he and other well know artists often played gigs in the bustling resorts along the Russian River. For Gene and his pals the warm nights by the silver river in the redwoods are memories still cherished today. Sipping the Bosso's wine in the soft moonlight, hustling the girls under the star sprinkled sky and "Dancin' with Anson". "It was wonderful," Gene smiled. "We lived at such a great time. We had so much fun together. I'll never forget it as long as I live."

CITY BALL

Kezar Stadium. circa 1940

X

"There was no place on earth like Kezar."

Bob St. Clair

To the generations of sports fans who have grown up since 1950 it is almost impossible to imagine college football without satellite TV, slow-motion replays and the ceaseless analysis of slick broadcasters. But in fact, long before TV nationalized the game – and many feel homogenized it to the point where it's difficult to distinguish one team from another – college football was a passionate part of America's sporting life.

The first intercollegiate football game was played on November 6, 1869 when a band of young men from Princeton University traveled down to New Brunswick, Connecticut to take on a group of students from Rutgers. Accounts vary, but it is widely held that after enjoying dinner, a game of billiards and a little girl watching – some things never change - the two teams removed their coats and ties and spent a couple of hours pushing and shoving each other in a match that resembled a mixture of soccer and rugby. With each goal valued at one point, the boys from Rutgers, with their red school scarves wrapped around their heads like turbans, were the first to score the required six goals and registered a 6-4 victory. From this inauspicious start American football grew into a national phenomenon. By the end of the 1920s renowned sportswriters like Ring Lardner and Grantland Rice had made young men like Red Grange, Jim Thorpe and a backfield from The University of Notre Dame called "The Four Horsemen" into an indelible and romantic part of the nation's folklore.

When Gene arrived in the fall of 1940 the bay area was saturated by no less that six college football teams, all of which played national schedules. Unlike the three larger schools; Stanford University, the University of California, and San Jose State, the three Catholic schools, St. Mary's College, Santa Clara University and the University of San Francisco, were too small to afford on campus stadiums. But the disparity ended there. Led by legendary coaches like Slip Madigan of St. Mary's and Buck Shaw of Santa Clara, the Catholic schools could compete with anyone, and played their games in two of the most unique stadiums in America.

Seal Stadium, "The Queen in Concrete"
Circa 1940

Erected in 1931 as a baseball park for the Pacific Coast League San Francisco Seals, Seal Stadium featured a modern lighting and public address system, seating capacity for 21,500 fans and cost $600,000 to build. Sitting at the corner of 16th and

Bryant streets the park - dubbed by fans as the "Queen in Concrete" - reigned over the northeast corner of the City's Mission District. Just a block away on 15th street stood the Wonder Bread Bakery and close by, on Shotwell Street, was the Holsum and California Baking Companies.

Besides the ballpark, the most dominant structure in the neighborhood was the Rainier Brewing Company that was located right next-door at 1550 Bryant Street. The brewery was one of about twelve in The City and, in the finest tradition, was a step below the trendy microbreweries of today both in clientele and in price. Its' most notable feature, and the one most remembered by all those who attended or played a game at Seal, was an enormous light display on the top of the building. Looming over the grandstand, the display depicted a huge beer mug that would slowly fill up with beer before being capped off with a perfect head and a lettered sign that flashed "Rainier" over the top of the glass. After it was full, the great mug would slowly drain down before filling up again with beer with a perfect head.

When the wind blew in off the bay, the park became a huge mixing bowl for the sounds and smells of the surrounding neighborhood. Between the scent of fresh cut grass and infield dirt, the pageantry and excitement of the game, the light show from the great beer mug, and the fantastic smells of the baking bread and the brewing beer, a night at Seal Stadium was a magnificent and memorable experience for players and fans alike.

On the other side of town stood another monument to The City's sporting scene. Upon her death in 1922, Mary H. Kezar sought to memorialize the memory of her mother and uncles, all of whom were pioneer residents of San Francisco. Toward that end, she bequeathed $100,000 to the City's Department of Parks, requesting that a suitable memorial be erected in their memory. The City's response was to kick in an additional $200,000 and hire an architect named Willis Polk to build a 60,000-seat stadium at the eastern end of Golden Gate Park. It is not clear if Polk was a sports fan, but it is pretty apparent that he was not much of an urban planner. Showing a great deal of faith in the city's public transportation system (either that or he thought the automobile was a passing fancy) he built parking spaces for a mere two hundred cars. And, with only 18,000 seats located between the goal lines, it also seems that he had a limited understanding of American football. At any rate, Kezar Stadium became the focal point of football in The City.

Standing approximately two miles from the Pacific Ocean, the huge concrete bowl was the natural home for squadrons of seagulls. The gulls tolerated fans and players on their turf during games, but always let their visitors know who was boss. "You could always tell who the veteran fans were," laughed one old timer. "When the gulls would fly up over the crowd, we'd always cover our heads with newspapers or our programs so we wouldn't get crapped on!"

Playing at Kezar was unforgettable and there is no one more qualified to comment on the experience than Bob St. Clair. A 1948 graduate of Poly High School (located across the street from Kezar and home to the Poly Parrots) Bob starred at USF before spending twelve All-Pro years with the San Francisco 49ers. A 1970 inductee in the National Football League Hall of Fame, the 6ft. 9in. former tackle played 189 games at the venerable old stadium and is the only man in America to have played his high school, college and professional football on the same field. When Kezar was remodeled in the 1990s city officials capped off Bob's historic career by naming the field in his honor. Still tough and fit, the strapping St. Clair smiles with stories and memories of the old stadium.

"There were many things about that place that stand out in my mind," he laughed. "Standing in the tunnel waiting to come on the field was one. The tunnel was at the East end of the stadium. It was really narrow and dark and wasn't paved so it was always real dusty. Both teams would stand crammed in there together waiting to go out on the field. In high school guys would start talking trash and we'd sometimes have fights in the tunnel."

"The stands were real close to the field," he went on. "You could hear everything. The aisles had steps so you could walk up to your seat, but the rest of the stadium just sloped up. When someone in the seats dropped something it slid all the way down to the bottom. People would drop cans and bottles and all kinds of stuff and you could hear it "ching chinging" off the metal seat posts all the way down."

"And you could really hear the fans," he went on. "If they didn't like you it was like they were right in your ear! With the fog, the sea gulls, the fans and the noise it was quite a place!"

GOLDEN DONS

Gene Benedetti, circa 1940.

XI

"Making history? Hell no. All we knew was we got the crap kicked out of us."

Joe Clerou

In the fall of 1924, under the guidance of coach Jimmy Needles, USF's (then St. Ignatius College) first football team made history when they were beaten 6-0 by a band of sailors from the naval destroyer USS Melville. The loss was the first of five in a winless inaugural season that ended with a 20-0 drubbing at the hands of the nearby Agnetian Club. But Needles, a gracious gentleman and fine teacher (who would claim distinction in 1936 when he coached America's first Olympic basketball team in Berlin) was competent and patient. By the time he relinquished his coaching duties to Lawrence "Spud" Lewis in 1932, he had built a powerful football program that competed on a national level. Lewis guided the Dons for five seasons, before giving way to George "Duke" Malley in 1936.

Under Malley, the Dons racked up 18 wins, 11 losses and 7 ties in four seasons. Malley's greatest day came in 1939 when his team became the first (and only) team in USF history to defeat archrival St. Mary's College. It was a huge win and when the Dons closed out the year with a convincing 26 -13 victory over Creighton University, school officials, fans and alumni held great expectations for the upcoming season.

Football at this level was a new world for Gene. The players were not only bigger and stronger but also much faster. The team played in major stadiums before huge crowds that generated enormous revenues. Games were broadcast live on the radio. Newspaper coverage was extensive, with sports writers covering the team on a daily basis. On the day after games, the local newspapers contained pages of images taken with a photographic device called "The Magic Eye" that shot the action on the field in a series of sequential pictures allowing readers to follow the game step-by-step. Players were publicly recognized by fans and students and became celebrities in the tight knit neighborhoods of The City. The overall result was a frenzied and glamorous mixture of business and big time sports.

"It was fun," said Gene. "I'd never been exposed to anything like that before. Of course the players were much better. I had played in the line in Junior college but when I got to USF all of the linemen averaged over 200 pounds. There was no way I could compete with those guys. But I was a good blocker so they made me a quarterback (blocking back) in the single wing. I didn't make first string, but I was on the team."

The Dons were scheduled to open the 1940 season against Stanford University. Four years earlier, the Indians had been the toast of the West coast when their famous "Vow Boys" (so called because they vowed never to lose to USC, which they had not) had capped off a string of three consecutive Rose Bowl appearances by beating Southern Methodist University 7-0 in 1936. But fortune proved a capricious mistress. By 1939 the bloom was off the Stanford rose and the once proud Indians had wilted into a band of woebegone losers. When they managed only one win over an anemic Dartmouth eleven, fans and alumni branded them the worst team in Stanford history and pressured school officials into firing coach Tiny Thornhill. Thus, as the Dons prepared for their season opener, there was little concern for the Indians.

"We were heavy favorites," remembered Gene. "They had been so lousy the year before and we had a strong team. They had won only one game, they had no new players and they'd fired their coach. We figured we'd beat the hell out of them."

But the previous spring Stanford had hired a new coach, and unbeknownst to Gene, and the football world at large, an Indian uprising that would make history was quietly brewing on the eucalyptus-lined practice fields down on The Farm.

Stanford fans and alumni viewed the hiring of Clark Shaughnessy as an act equivalent to throwing a bag of bricks to a drowning man. Their lament was not without reason. Despite the fact that he had been a coach for twenty-five years, Shaughnessy's mediocre record at Tulane, Loyola of New Orleans and the University of Chicago did little to assuage their concerns. Indeed, in his seven years at Chicago, where he had succeeded the immortal Amos Alonzo Stagg, his efforts had produced few wins and but one bright spot, when all-purpose running back Jay Berwenger won the first Heisman Trophy (at the time called the Downtown Athletic Club Trophy) in 1935. Other than Berwenger's achievement, success had eluded Shaughnessy. As a consequence, in 1939 when his hapless Maroons lost to Virginia 46-0, were beaten by Illinois 47-0, were dismantled by both Harvard and Ohio State by scores of 61-0, and throttled by Michigan 85-0, university president Dr. Robert Maynard Hutchins mercifully dropped the program, proclaiming; "I did not de-emphasize football … I abolished it!"

However, those within coaching circles held Shaughnessy in high regard, thinking of him as an eccentric genius who, if he ever found a way for his schemes to work, could potentially out shine them all. As a result, in the spring of 1940, when the taciturn Irishman arrived on the Stanford campus, both the uninformed and the enlightened were curious to see what he could do.

By any description Clark Shaughnessy was a man wrapped a little too tight. In the cigar smoking, hard drinking era of coach's and sportswriters of the 40s, the non-smoking teetotaler practiced a personal discipline akin to that of a monk. Standing 6 feet tall and weighing a fit 190 pounds, the 48-year old coach usually retired to bed around 7:00pm and, to the everlasting distress of his subordinates, rose before sunrise, refreshed and ready for work. So engrossed was he in the endless diagrams and formations swirling within his mind that it was common for him to forget the names of, or worse yet, to not even recognize his friends – never mind his players - on the street.

But peculiar or not, Shaughnessy understood the most fundamental of all coaching axioms, to wit; Do whatever is necessary to give your team a chance to win. He was also a keen judge of talent. When he studied the films of the 1939 Indians he realized that the players that flickered on the screen before him were not capable of success playing within the constraints of the offensive systems in vogue at the time. This team could win, he surmised, but only if they played to their strengths and were not asked to do something that they were not capable of. With that in mind, Shaughnessy reached deep into football antiquity, and pulled out an all but forgotten offense called the T-Formation.

Shaughnessy did not invent the T. In fact, Amos Alonzo Stagg had experimented with it before the turn of the century. But by the time Shaughnessy resurrected it, an entire generation of players and coaches had grown up having never heard of it. But before departing for Stanford, Shaughnessy had convinced his friend George Halas, coach of the Chicago Bears, of the T's vast potential and together they had installed the formation at the professional level. From that experience Shaughnessy felt confident that he could do the same at Stanford.

Very rare program from what many feel was the most historical college football game in history. It was also the only major college double header in Kezar Stadium history.

To grasp the significance of Shaughnessy's decision, one must understand that by 1940 American football had ossified into a game that was numbingly predictable. Nothing was new. Virtually every team in America used some variation of the single wing, (an offense invented by Pop Warner at the turn of the century) where the ball was snapped directly to a running back standing upright in the backfield, who either ran the ball or handed off to another running back. Advances were made behind a cordon of blockers three to four yards at a time. Defenses were rarely fooled, and passing the ball was the extreme exception.

In short, the game was stagnant, and, as expressed by Michigan coach Fielding "Hurry Up" Yost, extremely resistant to change. "There are no longer any distinctive systems in football," he declared before the 1940 season. "... there is only one formation that's any good and it's the single wing." Hence, within the context of the day, Shaughnessy's decision was radical and risky.

The veteran coach needed three elements if the offense he envisioned was to be successful. First, he needed intelligent players who were willing to try something new. Second, he needed a team with speed. And finally, a special athlete would be required to play quarterback.

L to R: Sammy Johnstone, Gene Benedetti, Pete Franceschi.

The first problem was easily solved. By definition Stanford students were a bright bunch, and after being hammered so viciously the year before, Shaughnessy reasoned that his new team would be willing to try anything. The issue of speed was also quickly resolved. Shaughnessy saw at once that the three primary running backs, Pete Kmetovic, Norm "Chief" Standlee, and Hugh "Duke" Gallarneau had the necessary size and quickness to not only run the middle of the field, but also to sweep the ends. But finding a quarterback was another matter. If the revolutionary offense was to prove successful, Shaughnessy needed a player with the skills of a magician, the courage of a lion and the swagger of a gunslinger. He found his man in a 5' 9" 170 pound junior from Glendale, California named Frankie Albert.

Albert was no stranger to success. When he was a senior at Glendale High School he had led his team to the 1937 Southern

California Championship. And, in his first year of college, he had led the Stanford freshman team to an undefeated season. But at the varsity level, he had vacillated between third and first string, causing observers to speculate that the diminutive left-hander was too small and slow for the grueling rigors of the college game. But Shaughnessy saw Albert as a perfect fit. "I knew he fitted exactly the requirements of the T-Formation," Shaughnessy wrote years later. "Frankie's talents were primarily those of a faker; he could fool people ... He was a poker player if ever there was one."

Shaughnessy first met his team in the spring of 1940.

"I remember it well," said Milt Vuninich (then a 19-year-old sophomore) in a 2002 interview. "He had us to a meeting in an empty classroom just off the quad. We were all sitting around wondering what he would be like. As soon as he walked in he commanded respect. He stood ramrod straight and was no nonsense."

After introducing himself, Shaughnessy turned and began to diagram a football formation on the classroom chalkboard.

"When he began to draw plays on the black board," Vuninich continued, "we immediately noticed that the line was balanced and that the quarterback was right up on the center – actually touching him. We had never seen anything like that before and as we watched him explain the 'T' all of us started to get excited."

"We were all interested," Vuninich went on. "Albert was really fascinated. When Coach was finished, he looked at all of us and said 'Boys, we are going to have a great team this year. If you learn this system well, it will take us to the Rose Bowl. So work hard. We are going to surprise a lot of people this year.'

"He commanded so much respect," Vuninich concluded. "We believed him. He dismissed the meeting and we got to work."

****

On Saturday, September 28, 1940 the sun rose from behind the Berkeley Hills to revel a beautiful San Francisco morning. Marble white clouds hung in a baby blue sky. Flocks of sea gulls floated over the bright blue bay. And the first traces of autumn blew across The City on the cool morning breeze. Down in Golden Gate Park, groundskeepers put the final touches of white chalk lines and yard markers on the freshly mowed field in Kezar Stadium. It was to be a glorious day for bay area football. For the first time in Kezar's fabled history a major college doubleheader was scheduled. Santa Clara was to play the University of Utah in the morning and the University of San Francisco would take on Stanford in the afternoon. Meanwhile across the bay, in a game considered much more momentous than the two at Kezar, the University of California's Golden Bears were expecting a sell-out crowd (a throng that would include a young man from Massachusetts named John F. Kennedy) to watch them play the Wolverines of Michigan and their great All America running back (and future Heisman Trophy winner), Tom Harmon.

The day began with Santa Clara defeating Utah 34-13 in the morning game before a crowd of about 40,000. As the contest wound down, Gene and the rest of his teammates finished dressing in the USF locker room before gathering to walk through the narrow tunnel that ran beneath the grandstand to the field.

"I was second string," Gene recalled. "I was not expecting to play, but I had never been in an environment like that before and it was very exciting."

Over in the Stanford dressing chamber, Clark Shaughnessy drew his team around him. "Men," he told them, "over in Berkeley today, a great player named Tom Harmon returned the opening kickoff 95 yards for a touchdown. He's a great All America player and played a great game today. And so will all of you. Now let's go!"

"He used Harmon's feat to motivate us," remembered Milt Vuninich. "We were all nervous wondering if our new offense would really work."

Life-long friend, Doc Haley.

The two teams emerged from the east tunnel and took the field about 3:30 pm. USF wore their familiar home uniforms; brownish gold pants, bright green jerseys with white numbers and black leather helmets. Stanford, on the other hand, made a more fashionable statement. To the surprise and delight of the fans, Shaughnessy had dressed his Indians in gaudy new uniforms; brilliant red jerseys with white numbers, spotless white pants, long red stockings, and white plastic helmets (something new at the time), all of which fairly gleamed in the bright afternoon sun.

After a brief warm-up, the captains met in the middle of the field for the toss of the coin. USF won and elected to receive.

The two teams lined up for the kickoff.

"We figured we'd beat them with no problem," recalled Gene. "I wasn't nervous, just excited. I was not supposed to play, so I figured I had a great seat to watch the game."

The contest began with each team unable to move the ball. After a rolling 61-yard Stanford punt drove the Dons into a hole the Indians held and forced the Dons to punt again. Over on the sideline, Gene watched as his teammates lined up and kicked the ball away.

Albert fielded the kick, and with the huge crowd roaring its approval, was tackled after a ten-yard gain. As the teams untangled themselves from the pile of bodies, an official blew his whistle and signaled for a time out. USF's starting quarterback Walt Puldoff was hurt and would have to leave the game.

As Puldoff was helped from the field, a USF coach turned to the bench: "Benedetti, you're in."

It was the moment Gene had dreamed of since his days on the sandlots of Cotati. With a rush of excitement he pulled on his helmet, buckled his chinstrap, and ran onto the field. From the floor of the stadium, the sounds and smells of the game swept over him. The pungent grass – cut short like a golf green, the fresh ocean breeze, the smell of leather from his shoulder pads and helmet and of course the great crowd; growling like a giant animal crouched in a thicket, waiting to erupt in a tumultuous roar. Down at the opposite end of the field, a flock of white sea gulls swooped down from the blue sky and landed in end zone. And over in the Stanford huddle, the scarlet clad Indians gathered around Frankie Albert and waited for the little quarterback to call their play.

What transpired next made football history.

"I can remember it as if it was yesterday," Gene said over sixty years later. "Stanford broke the huddle and came up to the line. We had scrimmaged against the single and double wing, and that's what we expected them to run. But they lined up in a 'T'. Albert stepped up and crouched under the center. We expected them to shift. But Frankie started barking out signals. Kmetovic went into motion one way and Gallarneau took off in the other direction. I had no idea what I was looking at. We had never seen anything like that before."

Clark Shaughnessy.

"Anyway," he chuckled, "Frankie kept calling out signals, took the snap, faked a handoff to Standlee, and faded back to pass. I never saw the ball because Albert had turned his back to me. I tackled Standlee, who carried me for about five yards, and thought I'd done a hell of a job. But he didn't have the ball! Albert had passed it to Gallarneau for a 17-yard gain!"

USF was in uncharted waters.

"I had no idea what to do," laughed Gene, "so I called time-out. In those days you couldn't leave the field during a time-out. Since I was playing quarterback, I was the automatic captain. We huddled up and all of the guys were looking at me and asking me what to do. Hell, I had no idea what to do. It was my first game! But I had to come up with something so I said, 'Let's go to a six man line, with three linebackers.' I told the two outside backers to cover the men in motion and as the middle backer I'd take anything up the middle. The two halfbacks were supposed to cover their ends man-to-man. I told the linemen to pinch in – I wanted to try and collapse them down toward the middle – and just cross the line of scrimmage and try and break up their plays."

It didn't work. By this time the Indians had recovered from a case of nerves, and the gears had started to mesh. Big Norm Standlee ripped off a twenty-yard gain through a hole the size of a canyon. Pete Kmetovic squirted through for another three yards. Now it was Standlee again, smashing the ball to the three-yard line. And a moment later, on a play where he was not touched, ("I don't think I even saw him," recalled Gene), Pete Kmetovic shot into the end zone for the games first touchdown. It was just the beginning. Like a young fighter tormenting a punch-drunk pug, the Indians ran, passed, blocked, tackled, and faked the heavily favored Dons with a dazzling impunity that left the crowd roaring with excitement. Albert was brilliant. So deft was his legerdemain with the football, and so deceptive were the plays that he called, that for the USF defense, it was like chasing crimson phantoms in a hurricane.

"Most of the time I never saw the ball," said Gene. "I kept tackling the first man through the line – in most cases it was Kmetovic or Standlee – and they never seemed to have the ball."

"You have to understand," he continued. "In those days, we were used to seeing the ball centered to a running back standing several yards behind the center. Even if someone tried a fake, we could see the ball. The idea was to push past the linemen and make the tackle. But with Stanford, Albert stood right up on the center and took the ball without showing it to us. By the time the ball carrier got to the line of scrimmage, he was going full speed and hardly needed a sustained block to make yardage."

"And, Albert faked so well," he went on. "He'd step one way and the back would step in another. We had never seen misdirection plays and it all happened so quick that we couldn't follow the ball. We were completely fooled. So were the coaches. We never had a chance. It was unbelievable."

The final score was 27- 0.

As is often the case, those who make history are seldom aware that they have done so. "We had no idea that we had done anything historical," said Milt Vuninich. "We were just elated that we had won. Of course that changed when we went undefeated and beat Nebraska the following January in the Rose Bowl."

The USF players also failed to grasp the significance of the contest.

"Their speed just killed us," recalled USF lineman Joe Clerou. "But making history? No. All we knew was that we got the crap kicked out of us!"

But in fact, the game had changed the way college football was to be played forever. Indeed, after Stanfords' victory on the national stage of the Rose Bowl, coaches all over the country turned to the T in droves. By the end of the decade, over seventy percent of the major colleges had adopted the system, and more were to follow.

While the game ultimately catapulted Stanford into national prominence, it sent the Dons reeling. In their next game at Kezar they lost to archrival St. Mary's 13-7 when a last minute interception was returned for a touchdown. And the following week, in a bitterly played night game at Seal Stadium, they blew a lead in the final three minutes and lost to San Jose State 7-6. The Dons picked up a little momentum in their next match when they played the tough Creighton University Blue Jays to a 0-0 tie. But the next week, when they folded in the second half against Buck Shaw's Santa Clara Broncos and were mauled 27-0, the season was in disarray.

But there were a few bright spots. For their sixth game of the season the team took to the road to play Hardin Simmons University. Located in the west Texas town of Abilene, HSU was a small Baptist college that played big time football producing players like All America and future NFL hall of famer, Clyde "Bulldog" Turner. In the 40s the Dons traveled by train – an adventure in itself – and school officials took care to see that road trips was enriching in ways other than just football. Hence, after a stop in Bakersfield, California, where they held practice on an abandoned baseball field, the train pulling the teams' private Pullman proceeded to the Northern Arizona town of Williams. It was Thanksgiving Day, and to celebrate the holiday the boys detrained and boarded a chartered bus bound for the Grand Canyon. The fifty-mile drive through the rugged snow-covered country was one of spectacular beauty for the city kids, most of who had never been away from home and only a few of whom had ever seen snow. The Canyon of course, was spectacular and Thanksgiving dinner even better.

"We had Thanksgiving dinner at the El Tovar," smiled Gene. "That place was something, I'll tell you. You should have seen it!" Designed by architect Charles Whittlesey and perched just twenty feet from the edge of the Canyons South Rim, the El Tovar (named for Don Pedro Tovar, a Spanish explorer who first learned of the Canyons existence) was built in 1905 by the Santa Fe Railroad. Springing from the very rocks of the canyon itself, the building was a rustic blend of Swiss, Scandinavian and American architecture. Staffed by renowned railroad concessionaire Fred Harvey, the dining room offered breathtaking views, excellent food, and sparkling service from his famous white –smocked and wholesome "Harvey Girls."

"I'll always remember that day, said Gene. "The Jesuits really went first class when it came to travel. It was really beautiful. After we ate we all went out and made snowballs and threw them at each other. Most of the guys had never seen snow. Our punter, Cliff Fisk, kicked a ball down into the Canyon. One of the reporters "measured" it and said it set a record. But mostly we just looked at the magnificent scenery. I remember thinking how lucky I was and how much fun it was. The whole day was a great experience."

It was indeed. As the team held a short practice before climbing back on the train, reporter Bob Stevens captured the essence of the moment; "It was a unique picture," he wrote to the folks back home, "27 kids in the green and white uniforms of the Dons, slushing around on a background of a million diamonds."

After stopping the next day for a final workout in Lubbock Texas, the train arrived the following morning in the village of Buffalo Gap, where the boys were transferred to private cars for the 14-mile drive to Abilene's Paramore Field on the Hardin Simmons Campus.

The arrival of a team from the West Coast was a signature event in the tiny west Texas city. The local press put a large picture of both squads on the front page of the morning paper and duly noted that two extra telegraph lines had been installed in the stadium press box to accommodate the national reporters who were traveling with the Dons. The papers also advised fans that a large crowd was expected for the Homecoming event and, in a quaint small town touch, informed readers that advance tickets were available at Ward's Hilton pharmacy.

The game itself was a disappointment. "The weather was terrible," remembered Gene. "I never knew it could get that cold and windy in Texas. We had a pretty good punter, but when he kicked the ball it was so windy that it went straight up in the air. The rain actually turned to sleet! I had never been so cold!" But the Cowboys were accustomed to playing under the gray, lighting shattered skies. With players like quarterback Owen Goodnight and fullback Moon Mullins leading the charge, they hammered the Dons 28-18 before 3,000 shivering fans on the frigid wind swept plains.

"We got beat," laughed Gene. "But hell, it was fun to take the trip. I had never done any traveling before, and I'll never forget it."

The Dons next game was also on the road. "We went down to Los Angeles to play Loyola," smiled Gene. "That was a real first class trip. We stayed at the Hollywood Roosevelt Hotel. What an experience that was."

Stationed like a proud conquistador across the street from Grauman's Chinese Theater, (with its legendary forecourt with the footprints of the stars) the Hollywood Roosevelt defined the glamour of Hollywood's gilded age. Opened in 1927, the Spanish Colonial edifice was known as "The Home of the Stars" and to stay there was to visit Tinsel Town's front room. At one time or another, luminaries like Clark Gable, Douglas Fairbanks Jr., F. Scott Fitzgerald, and Ernest Hemmingway, just to name a few, called the Roosevelt home. The place fairly oozed with history. In 1929 the first Academy Awards ceremony (originally called the Merit Awards) was held in the fabulous Blossom Room. During the prohibition years, Errol Flynn made bathtub gin in the back of the hotels barber shop. And on the tiled steps of the magnificent lobby, beneath the two-story ceiling painted like a secular Sistine Chapel, Bill "Bojangles" Robinson showed a little girl named Shirley Temple his famous dance steps. For Gene it was a dazzling experience. "I'd never seen anything as fancy in my life," he said. "It was a long way from the ranch."

Loyola University played their home games at Gilmore Stadium. Built by E.B. Gilmore in 1934, the 18,000 seat bowl was located just off the corner of 3rd and Fairfax streets on the site presently occupied by the CBS television studios. Known as "the working mans' stadium" Gilmore was the first venue built for midget auto racing and was part of a complex that not only contained the world famous Farmers Market but also Gilmore Field, the home of the Pacific Coast Leagues' Hollywood Stars baseball club. The stadium was ideal for its versatility and became the site of many notable sporting events. In 1934 a Three Stooges movie entitled "Three Little Pigskins" (co-starring a young actress named Lucille Ball in the role of a gangster's moll) was filmed there with the Loyola football team appearing as extras. Fortunately for USF, the 1940 Lions were little better than the ones who served as the Stooges foil. As a result, the Dons registered their first win of the season by pounding the woeful Loyolaians 21-0.

On the following Saturday, the long season finally came to a close when the high-flying Red Raiders of Texas Technological College rolled into Kezar. Sporting a record of eight wins against only one loss, the Raiders were billed as the best dressed team in the Southwest and practically glowed in the dark with their bright uniforms of scarlet and black silk adorned with huge white numerals "so their Mammas and Daddy's could see their boys out there." Led by the lovable Peter "Petey" Cawthon and his assistant Russell "Dutchy" Smith, two flamboyant coaches who prowled the sidelines shouting at the top of their lungs and praying for relief and redemption, playing the Red Raiders was like attending a gridiron revival and salvation show. But the tough kids from the west Texas oilfields could play. And on this cold and muddy day at Kezar they meant to close out the year as winners against the hapless Dons.

USF, on the other hand, had trouble fielding a team. "Half of our guys were in bed with the flu," remembered Gene. "We didn't know if we'd have anyone left to play." But on game day the Dons gamely crawled from their sickbeds, took the field inspired and played what reporters called the best game of the year when, fighting hard, they lost a thrilling 23-21 contest on a last second field goal.

Thus ended Gene Benedetti's first season in the bright lights of big time college football. Despite the teams dismal record it had been a notable year. The historic Stanford game, the cross-country trip to Texas, the majestic pinnacles of the Grand Canyon, and the glitz and glamour of Hollywood had all served to take a little country out of the boy from Cotati.

"I had a great time," he said fondly. "I guess it would have been better if we had won more. But looking back it had been so much fun. And what the hell, that's what it's all about."

PRELUDE TO INFAMY

1940 Navy recruiting poster.

XII

"We just read the sports pages and comics . . . "

Gene Benedetti

It was now the end of 1940 and the war in Europe had been raging for over a year. To America's leaders it seemed as if the walls were closing in. In response Congress passed two pieces of legislation that had an immediate impact. First, in November, President Roosevelt signed the Lend Lease Bill, making 7 billion dollars available to England for war materiel and other aid. The bill also allowed the U.S. Navy to escort supply convoys across the North Atlantic, in effect putting the United States in an undeclared war with Germany. Hitting even closer to home was the Selective Service Act (signed in late 1940) making all males between the ages of eighteen and thirty-five eligible for America's first peacetime draft. The results were an immediate wake up call for millions of young men who were required to register for induction into the armed forces. In order to avoid conscription many men, including Gene's older brother Dante, volunteered. "Dan went early," said Gene. "He enlisted in the Navy and ended up in pre-flight at Oakland California and then on to Corpus Christi, Texas for flight school."

Meanwhile across the Atlantic, England, proud and unbowed after surviving the terrible bombing of the Battle of Britain, was going it alone as she tenuously hung on to her island. Across the stormy English Channel, Germany held sway over virtually the entire continent. The situation was dire. On June 22, 1941 when Hitler's vast armies turned east and thundered into Russia, it looked as if nothing could stop them. But Europe was only part of the problem. Far to the east the Empire of Japan was growing restless. And the samurai sword that she rattled was ominous indeed.

Unlike Germany and Italy no single dictator had emerged in Japan to seize power. Ruled by an emperor who was considered divine, and inhabited by a people steeped in antediluvian and mysterious traditions, Japans' road to oppression had been gradual. In the 87 years since Commodore Matthew Perry had dropped anchor in Tokyo bay, the Japanese had transformed their country into a major industrial and military power strong enough to defeat Russia in the Russo-Japanese War of 1905.

But technological advances notwithstanding, Japan remained a nation with few natural resources. In order to remain powerful, her leaders sought an empire beyond the isolation of her home islands. Toward that end in September 1931, she attacked and conquered the Chinese province of Manchuria and installed a puppet state called Manchukuo. By 1937 she had signed the Anti-Comintern Pact with Germany (Italy became a signatory a year later) and with the support and encouragement of Europe's fascists states continued her conquest of China. The Japanese were cruel and ruthless. In December 1937, when the rape of the city of Nanking resulted in the indiscriminate slaughter of over 350,000 innocents, the world was appalled and horrified. By 1938 Japan controlled China's entire coastline and had begun to look east toward the vast riches of the Pacific. Her subsequent invasion of French Indochina (present day Viet Nam) in 1940 was a final match to the fuse. In response, President Roosevelt froze Japans assets and cut off all exportation of scrap iron, steel and aviation fuel.

Although the headlines screamed with these events Americans still found it difficult to connect with the war. "It was all so distant," said Gene. "Remember, there was no TV or anything like that to give us a sense of urgency. To us the war was just black and white pictures in the paper. And besides, we usually read the sports page and the comics and got on with our daily lives."

EVELYN

XII

"She was stunningly beautiful."

Jim Bligh

Across the country in Washington DC, Cus Pirro was wrapping up a busy year. After graduating from Catholic University the previous spring, he applied and was accepted at CU's law school. To help defray expenses, the rugged lineman earned a few extra dollars playing semi-professional football with the Portsmouth Cubs in the Dixie Football League (a part-time job he pursued the following season with the Richmond Rebels), while working on campus as CU's freshman basketball coach and director of intramural athletics. Cus's roommate that year was a local kid from DC named Joe Rattigan. "We lived together on campus," Rattigan recalled. "I had a Knights of Columbus scholarship and Cus had worked a deal with the school where he coached basketball in exchange for his tuition and room. It was a good deal."

Despite the demands of his coaching duties and academic commitments, Cus managed to find time for a social life. One night that spring - the exact place and details are lost in time - he and a few pals decided to attend a local dance.

"He was really a good looking guy," recalled Rattigan. "The girls fell all over him."

Ida Pirro concurred: "He was very handsome" she said sixty years later. "He was about 6'3 with dark hair and had beautiful high cheekbones. He always reminded me of an Indian brave."

Evelyn - 3rd row, second from right with white shoes - at John Burroughs Junior High School.

But on this night things were different. It was Cus's turn to fall, and fall he did when his eyes met those of a beautiful brunette across the room.

Evelyn Frances Birrel was born on September 14, 1921 in Washington D.C. She was the first of two daughters born to Gordon and Marian Birrel. Her father's parents, Scottish born Rev. Mathew Brown Birrel and his wife, New Hampshire born Frances House Catlin (who was related to the famous frontier painter George Catlin) were missionaries in service to the Christian Missionary Alliance. Spending virtually their entire lives in Foreign Service, this courageous and devout couple had met and married in the mission fields of China where Gordon and his three sisters were born and reared. As a lad growing up in the rugged Chinese countryside of the early twentieth century, Gordon's boyhood was one of sustained adventure. When he came of age, his parents sent him to the states to attend Wheaton College in rural Illinois. But in 1916 World War One was raging and driven by the zeal of youth and British patriotism; (since his father was a Scotsman Gordon held British citizenship) young Gordon left the little Wesleyan college in the farmlands and volunteered for the Canadian Expeditionary Force. He was sent overseas where he fought in the horrors of the trenches. The dark experience changed him forever. By the time he returned home, his priorities were to marry, raise a family, and enjoy the blessings of each day. Toward that end, he settled in the Washington, DC area where he married Marian and took a job as a controller for the National Correspondence College, a position from which he retired. Gordon was a lifetime learner. After his retirement, he went on to earn a masters degree in economics and become a professor at the University of Baltimore. Quiet, erudite, and kind, Gordon (whom

Evelyn's Mother, Marian Bowers Birrel.

his grandchildren called Topah) was a fine man, a sensitive and talented poet, and a loving and supportive father.

"One of my best memories as a child was when he took me to see the Ringling Brothers Circus," smiled Evelyn. "I was surprised that Mom let us do it. I loved it. I loved the animal acts, and seeing them in their cages. It is a wonderful memory."

Evelyn's mother, Marian Bowers (whom the kids called Tomah), was also from a deeply religious home. Inclined toward music, she was a talented pianist, and lovely vocalist. When Evelyn was young, Marian paid for piano lessons for both she and her younger sister Barbara Anne (whom everyone called Bobbi). It must be said, however, that Bobbi took to the task much better that Evelyn. "I was very lazy," she laughed years later. "Bobbi could play beautifully, and I used to fan her and mother on the warm days while they played."

In contrast to her husband, Marian was very serious when it came to religion. Indeed, seldom was the Sunday that she did not take the girls to one of the non-denominational churches in the area or to various outdoor "camp meetings" where she played the organ and sang for the small congregations.

"I liked taking communion at church," remembered Evelyn. "I got to have a sip of grape juice."

The rustic camp meetings, however, were a different story.

"They had out houses with a Sears catalog for toilet paper," she winced. "I hated them."

Marian also imposed strict protestant discipline on her daughters, denying them worldly pleasures like reading the funny papers, and going to the movies. While she was growing up, Evelyn's best friend was a beautiful little girl from across the street (and later across town) named Betty O'Brien. Betty was Irish and

Catholic - shortcomings that Marian tolerated - and attended Sacred Heart Catholic School. In spite of any religious differences however, Betty and Evelyn become the best of pals.

"I used to love to visit her," recalled Evelyn. "When we were together, I could read the funny papers, and we could also go to the movies!"

Betty was also concerned for her little friend's soul.

"When we were about five years old Betty "baptized" me as a Catholic in the bathtub," laughed Evelyn. "For the rest of our lives she never let me forget that she had "saved" me."

After attending John Burroughs Grammar School, Evelyn entered McKinley Technical High School in Washington. Founded in 1884, McKinley was the flagship of Washington's public high schools. Renowned for its high academic standards, championship track teams, and crack Cadet Corps Drill Team, McKinley offered a wide variety of classes and an active campus life. Evelyn excelled in English, History and Journalism, graduating in 1938 with a fine secondary education.

"I loved to write," she recalled. "I had received an award for writing in Junior High School, and by the time I graduated from McKinley, I wanted to attend Columbia University in New York and major in journalism."

But the family's financial position was limited.

"There was not enough money for me to go to Columbia," she said. "Instead, I decided to attend the Washington School for Secretaries."

There was nothing subordinate about her decision. Located in the Press Building on Fourteenth Street in the heart of the capitol, the Washington School for Secretaries was very upscale. Offering a demanding and comprehensive course for young ladies intent on becoming professional secretaries, the one-year curriculum included classes in typing, card catalog, and shorthand. It was very disciplined. Early pictures depict well-dressed young ladies, sitting in neat rows behind old-fashioned typewriters, under the watchful eye of sever looking instructors. The school was well respected in town and it was from the ranks of its graduates that many congressional offices recruited their clerical help.

"I did very well there," said Evelyn. "I got all A's and could type 115 words per minute. After I graduated in the spring of 1939, I was asked to work at a convention in the Commerce Building in Washington. I'll never forget it. I was so excited at the prospect of working that I bought my first pair of white gloves!"

Apparently Evelyn's white-gloved performance at the U.S. Steel booth drew some attention.

"My job was to take down the names of anyone who was interested in U.S. Steel," she remembered. "I did well and met many people. After the convention, they asked me to work for them. It was all very flattering and I took the job."

As a consequence, by the time she and her girlfriend Ruby stepped out to go dancing that spring evening, Evelyn Birrel had become the quintessential career women of the day. Bright, young and single she was employed by one of the largest corporations in the world and living in the most glamorous of capitol cities. She was also stunningly beautiful. When asked about the night she met Cus Pirro she smiled and said simply; "We looked at each other one time and that was it".

SENIOR YEAR

Senior Picture; USF class of 1942

XIV

***"It has been a great journey, a splendid one . . .
the countless good times together
that neither war nor peace will ever completely succeed in erasing . . ."***

"The Adios" USF class of 1942

Back in San Francisco the summer of 1941 cooled to autumn as Gene moved back to The City for his senior year at USF. Academically, he was on track to graduate the following spring, and athletically, he was looking forward to his final year of football. While the prior season had been enlightening and fun the end result had been disappointing. As he unpacked his bags in the new Varsity House on Stanyan Street, he was hoping for a better year. He had reason to be optimistic. In the off-season university officials, intent on improving the schools football fortunes, had reached beyond the bay area and hired a new coach to replace the departed George Malley.

Newell "Jeff" Cravath arrived on the Hilltop with an impressive gridiron pedigree. As a 1926 graduate of the University of Southern California, he had earned All America honors as a rugged hard-hitting center under the great Howard Jones. After successful coaching stints with the Trojan frosh and the University of Denver, he had returned to USC where he served under Jones as line coach. Married and father to two daughters, the bespectacled thirty-seven year old mentor who liked to be called "Jeff", was a skilled teacher, a strict disciplinarian and an unyielding fundamentalist. By the time he signed with USF he had four Rose Bowls to his credit, and fans and alumni were hopeful that he could lead the Dons to respectability. When he and his assistant, Bill Howard, also from USC, gathered their team for their first scrimmage in mid September, the players were immediately impressed.

"He really worked us," said Gene. "But we needed it. And he was such a great teacher. He was very thorough. He made sure you understood what he was taking about. He instilled confidence in us from the first day of practice. I learned more from him and Bill Howard in that one year than I did from all of my years in football put together."

Jeff Cravath, Don's coach.

But Cravath was nothing if not realistic and realized that after the debacle of the year before, the road to respectability would be a long one. Accordingly, when local odds makers installed his team as a four to one underdog for their season opener against Santa Clara, all he could do was vow to reporters; "… we'll have a ball team by the end of the year …"

Thus instilled with a new attitude, and adorned in new uniforms of emerald green jerseys, with bright gold numerals and flashy pants of "butter silk" gold, USF opened the 1941 season against Buck Shaw's ball club before 40,000 raucous fans at Kezar. Unfortunately, attitude and raiment weren't enough to stave off the Bronco's who outclassed the still adjusting Dons by a score of 32-7. Undaunted and patient, coach Cravath kept teaching. And the boys kept learning. Their mutual diligence paid off the following week, when, despite several starters being out with the flu, they managed a hard fought 13-7 victory over future all-pro Marion Motley and his University of Nevada Wolf Pack in a night game at Seal Stadium. With their record now even, odds makers rated their next game with St. Mary's a toss-up. But on October 12th the flush of the prior week's victory turned to a burning embarrassment when the Gaels dismantled the Dons 30-0 behind the fabulous passing of sophomore Johnny "Presto" Podesto.

Senior football, 1941

Stanford University was up next. To prepare for the defending Rose Bowl champions, Cravath took the team inside where he commandeered the buildings office chairs and arranged them in a

'T' formation. Using the chairs as a sort of rolling diagram, the innovative coach drilled his charges in the various nuances of the complicated system. It would have worked - had the boys remembered to tackle. But, sadly, that was not the case, as Shaughnessy's Indians toyed with the Hilltoppers, handing them a 42-26 loss before a crowd of 60,000 at Stanford Stadium.

Three Big men on campus; L to R: Gene, Tiger Smith, and Doc Haley.

The Stanford game proved to be a watershed for the Dons. Indeed they had scored 26 points against a tough defense (some of them behind the "swell" blocking of Gene Benedetti) and although they had lost, savvy observers recognized that they were finally coming together.

Their progress was evident the following Friday night when BYU's Cougars roared into Seal Stadium - only to limp out three hours later on the short end of a 25-13 score. The win boosted the boy's confidence. With their record now at 2 wins and 3 losses fan support was also on the rise. Consequently, when on the following Saturday, over 400 students and alumni traveled down to Fresno, set up a Green and Gold Headquarters at the Hotel California, and – to the mortification of locals citizens - took to the streets singing the USF fight song at the top of their lungs, expectations were high. The Dons did not disappoint. In a wild shoot out, they set an all time USF scoring record by blasting Jimmy Bradshaw's Bulldogs 47-27 before 19,000 screaming fans at sold out Ratcliffe Stadium. A highlight of the evening was the Bulldog band that entertained the multitudes with a half-time "light show" wherein their instruments were trimmed with neon piping as they paraded across the darkened field in the balmy valley night.

With their record now even, the Dons went on a three-week tear, whipping Loyola 27-20 on the road at Gilmore (another rowdy road trip for the fans who rode the Southern Pacific "Coaster" to the game), shutting out San Jose State 20-0 at Seal Stadium and beating Fort Ord's cadre of soldiers 21-13 at Kezar. The string of five straight victories not only captivated The City's football fans, but also made the Dons darlings of the local media, causing more than one writer to note that Cravath had indeed forged "... a ball team by the end of the year ..." The writers went on to speculate that if the Dons could replay their losses, the outcome could well be a different story. Hence with one game to go, sports fans all over The City were buzzing with excitement as they eagerly awaited the arrival of the Dons final opponent.

A FLASH OF BLOND & INNOCENCE LOST

Taken on December 6, 1941 just hours before the attack at Pearl Harbor. Billy Jack "Spook" Murphy breaks into the clear as Gene Benedetti closes in for the tackle. Courtesy Mississippi State Universtity archives.

XV

"It was the last time we were all together."

Gene Benedetti

Of all the teams that visited San Francisco in the pre-war years there were few better, and none more colorful than the 1941 Mississippi State College Maroons. With only one loss against an otherwise perfect record, these proud sons of the South were the defending Orange Bowl champions, winners of the vaunted Southeastern Conference and fresh off a stunning upset victory over their hated archrival, Ole Miss. According to their advance agent Max Patrick, who arrived in town three days before his team to hype the game, the Maroons were - "lookin forward suh, to playin ya'll heah in Frisco by the Bay."

Patrick went on to express regret that Mississippi's two bands would not be making the trip, explaining that his school featured two musical organizations; one a marching band that played traditional martial music, and the other a less conventional ensemble that sat in the stands and belted out a pulsating southern boogie-woogie from whistle to gun.

"No self-respectin' southern team," he drawled, "would dream of takin' the field without proper music." "But," he went on, "we do have coupla ol' boys that'll run rat down yer throat if ya'll give 'em a chance."

They did indeed have a couple of boys who could run, and the swiftest of them all was a strapping six-foot 195 pound junior from the tiny country town of Philadelphia, Mississippi named John T. "Blondy" Black.

In an era when men played in high-top shoes and ran on dirt tracks, Blondy Black stood alone. Billed as "the fastest man in America to run the length of a football field", the handsome broad-shouldered junior ran the 100-yard dash in a world-class time of 9.6 seconds and was often compared to Olympic Silver Medallist, Ralph Metcalf.

"Ya'll are gonna like what you see," drawled agent Patrick. "Ol' Blondy can really fly."

With their aw shucks pass the biscuits manners, their ferocious attack-em-from-anywhere-on-the-field style of play, and their veins coursing with the rhythm of a southern juke joint, playing against the raw-boned farmers from Starkville was a spicy taste of the dash and élan of Dixie.

The Maroons rolled into The City on Thursday December 4, 1941, to a reception worthy of visiting royalty. After a series of welcome speeches by city and school officials, Coach Allyn McKeen graciously thanked his hosts before checking his team into the Whitcomb Hotel at Eighth and Market Streets. The next day, after a brief sightseeing tour (including the obligatory cable car ride) the soft-spoken southerner hustled his team out to the privacy of Kezar Stadium for a late afternoon workout. It had rained all week in The City, and the breeze off the ocean was crisp and cold as the players jogged on the damp grass and prepared for the upcoming contest the following afternoon. Up in the silent stands a few reporters, along with some of the USF players, watched the workout in the chilly gloam of the empty stadium. Across the park, the sun slipped beyond the orange vermilion towers of the Golden Gate Bridge. And farther out to sea, beyond the distant horizon, the cold winds of a terrible war made their way towards a sleeping America.

****

The two teams took the field on Saturday December 6, 1941 before a crowd of 40,000. It was a splendid winter day. After a week of rain The City gleamed like a polished diamond in the bright December sun. Mississippi State – after arriving at the stadium in grand fashion aboard a city fire truck - wore their road uniforms of maroon pants with white stripes, maroon shirts with white numerals and black helmets. USF was attired in their traditional jerseys of Kelly green with gold numbers, black helmets, and their now familiar pants of butter silk gold. The turf was still soft and damp from the rain. Up in the stands the student card section - under the direction of seniors Mal McCarthy and Jim Grealish - surged with enthusiasm as they raised their cards and spelled out "Hi Pop" to the crowd across the way. It was Father's Appreciation Day and Gene glowed with

Blondy Black.

pride at the sight of Giacondo sitting on the sidelines with the rest of the Dads.

"It was a little uncomfortable for him," he recalled. "He didn't speak English and felt out of place. But I was glad that he was there. He had never seen me play at USF and I really appreciated him being there."

The great "Blondy Black" eludes USF's Lee Borges before exploding up the north sideline for an 83 yard touchdown.

The game was a barnburner. Mississippi State scored two touchdowns in the first quarter on sharp blocking and scorching runs by Blondy Black and Billy Jack "Spook" Murphy. The Dons struck back with an unchecked ferocity of their own.

"Early in the game," recalled halfback Charlie White, "Blondy Black broke through the line and Phil Kearny met him head on in a tremendous hit. I swear you could hear the crack of the collision throughout the entire stadium. It was a very tough game and Blondy was all they said he was"

In the second quarter Black continued to live up to his billing when, after being pushed back with a 15 yard penalty, he lined up in punt formation, faked to his left and exploded 83 yards up the north sideline for an electrifying touchdown.

"We had never seen speed like that," said Gene shaking his head at the memory. "My God he was good. He was big and tough. He broke my nose twice that day … pushed it from one side of my face to the other. He was the best I ever played against. The best I ever saw."

The Dons scored once before the half, and the two teams each scored once more in the fourth quarter to bring the crowd to its feet in a thunderous display of appreciation for the fine effort from both ball clubs. Finally, with the score 26-13 in favor of the southerners, the black hand and the red hand on the great clock at the east end of the stadium came together. It was over. In a warm display of respect and sportsmanship, the weary athletes shook hands in the middle of the field and walked together through the tunnel back to the dressing rooms.

Blondy Blacks's roommate, Lamar Blount. "We were just a bunch of country boys who had never been anywhere. Coming to San Francisco was the biggest trip of our lives."

"It was my last game," said Gene, "and it was a great one. Even though we lost, it had been a great game and a great year. Looking back on my life, I never had so much fun than when I was a football player."

After the game Gene and some of the players went down to the Palace Hotel on Market Street.

"We met a few of the Mississippi players for a few drinks before they left on the train," he said. "They were really a great bunch of guys … great players too. Blondy Black, Billy Jack Murphy, Lamar Blount, … all just great guys."

Later that night the boys drove to teammate Charlie White's house out in the avenues for a party. "We had a fine time," said Gene. "It was a wonderful party. All of the guys were there, Doc Haley, Bebe Moore, Tiger Smith, Butch Burtner, Vic Ramus, Mal McCarthy, everybody. We had barbeque and drinks and stayed up all night. It was our last night of innocence. It was the last time we were all together."

****

Flying at 9,800 feet above the Pacific, Commander Mitsuo Fuchida saw the first rays from the rising sun filter through the clouds and gleam celestially off the wings of his aircraft. For the thirty-nine year old aviator it was an omen - proof that a divine presence had blessed the grim work that he and the crewmen of the ten sections of high-level bombers that flew in triangular formations behind him were about to perform. As flight commander of 180 warplanes, Fuchida had taken off from the black deck of the Japanese carrier Akagi just before sunrise. Under the command of Vice Admiral Chuici Nagumo, the Akagi was the flagship of the Imperial Japanese Navy's Air Fleet One, a task force of thirty war ships that stood to sea eleven days earlier when they slipped out of fog shrouded Hitokappu Bay in the Kuril Islands. After a skilled and stealthy cruise of nearly 4,000 miles, the deadly armada had arrived undetected at its pre-assigned attack position 200 miles north of Oahu. And there in the pre-dawn darkness, Nagumo had turned his six aircraft carriers into the eastern wind and launched Operation Hawaii, the attack on the United States Fleet at Pearl Harbor.

As the sun continued its ascent in the tropical sky, Fuchida saw the island of Oahu jump into view. It was beautiful. Like a rugged uncut emerald trimmed in white surf, it rose from its setting of deep blue and beckoned the silver bombers that roared toward its northern shore. Fuchida moved his plane to the front of the formation and led the streaking attackers through the mist enshrouded mountains. And suddenly, there it was – Pearl Harbor, home to the American Fleet that lay serenely at anchor on this quiet Sabbath morning. The senior aviator smiled with satisfaction, clicked on his radio, and gave the order that plunged a sleeping America into infamy.

SUNDAY DECEMBER 7, 1941
SAN FRANCISCO

USF goes to war.

XVI

"We wanted to fight em!"

Gene Benedetti

"I awoke to the sound of a newspaper boy yelling 'Extra! Extra!,'" said Gene of that fateful morning. "We'd all stayed out late at the party. When we got back to the Varsity House on Stanyan Street, I'd opened a window before I went to sleep. When I heard the kid yelling I knew it was something significant. We never got an 'Extra!' out where we lived. I slipped on a pair of pants, went downstairs and bought a Sunday paper. I still remember reading the paper in disbelief. At that moment, my life changed forever."

The Japanese had attacked a nation sharply divided. On the one hand, isolationists strongly felt that, while it was bearable for America to aid her allies, vis-à-vis programs like Lend Lease, War Bonds, and Bundles for Britain; it was not acceptable to risk American boys to fight in a foreign conflict. In contrast, political realists, led by President Roosevelt, realized that war in Europe was unavoidable. Japan's aggressiveness would have to be dealt with, and legislation like Lend Lease and the Selective Service

Act was but a prelude to the inevitable. On the street, most Americans were opposed to participation in the European war, failed to see Japan as a threat and were woefully uninformed. All of this changed in the smoke and carnage of Pearl Harbor.

As news of the disaster flashed across the nation, Americans reacted immediately. Hours after the first bombs fell on battleship row, frightened San Franciscans gathered at the seashore to gaze at the horizon in search of the Japanese fleet. Naval and Coast Guard vessels laid mines under the Golden Gate Bridge. A national state of emergency was declared. All service men were recalled to their bases. That night, a black out was imposed over the entire west coast as people fitfully wondered where the "Japs" would hit next.

"No one knew what to do," said Gene. "At school the next day we all just stood around trying to figure out what to do. We were all angry. We wanted to fight 'em! My parents, of course, were very concerned. By that time my brother Dan was in Navy flight school in Texas. We didn't know what would happen to him. And we didn't know what would happen to us. It was very frightening."

The reaction at USF was typical of colleges throughout the country.

"Following Pearl Harbor, USF literally went to war," noted University Archivist Fr. Michael Kotlanger S.J. "The focus on campus changed overnight. Instead of academic and recreational activities, campus life was defined by the draft, enlistment, call to report for duty, and the constant departure of young men for boot camp. In all, several hundred students, graduates and faculty members went off to serve in the military, including several Jesuits who went as chaplains."

"It was all pretty confusing at first," recalled Gene. "Our main focus was trying to decide what branch of the service to join. The Army set up a quartermaster program for those who wanted to sign up. The guys on campus who were in the ROTC were already in as part of the Coastal Defense Battalion. The Marines had their Platoon Leaders Class. We spent a lot of time making decisions, getting transcripts together, getting physicals – that kind of stuff."

"We were all subject to the draft," he went on. "But I didn't want to wait for that. I wanted to get overseas. There was no bravery about it. I just wanted to do my part. Everyone felt the same way. We wanted to do something fast. So Doc Haley, Mal McCarthy and I went down and signed up for the Marines"

Gene's enthusiasm notwithstanding, joining up was not that easy.

"I'll never forget it," he said ruefully. "We went down to the Federal Building and took our physicals. The school was going to let us graduate early and we were all set to head out to Quantico, Virginia for Officers' Candidate School. We had a big farewell party at Milli and Red's house up on Wallace Court in Petaluma. It was really a great party. All the guys from school came up. The next morning I was dealing with my hangover and getting ready to go down to The City, when a telegram arrived telling me I was unqualified for the Marine Corps because of a medical problem."

"I was crushed," he went on. "I went down to The City anyway to find out what happened. As it turned out, our team doctor, old Doc Sooy, who had given me my Marine Corps physical had failed me because of a calcium deposit in my leg. I didn't know what to do so I went and saw my old coach, Jeff Cravath.

He agreed that my leg was fine, but knew that the Doctor wouldn't budge."

"Anyway," he continued, "Cravath told me that Gene Tunney was in town interviewing candidates for his physical fitness program in the Navy. He offered to call him for me. I said 'sure' and before I knew it, I was sitting in front of the great Gene Tunney interviewing for his program."

James Joseph "Gene" Tunney was one of the most colorful characters to emerge from the roaring 20's. Reared in a working class neighborhood, Tunney had learned to fight in the streets of New York City. When the United States entered WWI in 1917, he enlisted in the Marines, went overseas to France and returned as the light heavy weight boxing champion of the American Expeditionary Force. Known thereafter as The Fighting Marine, Tunney became the heavy weight champion of the world when he defeated the great Jack Dempsey in 1926. In a controversial rematch, Tunney successfully defended his crown as beneficiary of "The Long Count", a legendary incident in boxing history in which Dempsey was penalized for not going to a neutral corner after knocking Tunney down. The extra time allowed the champ time to rise from the canvas, clear his head, and win the match.

Astute, intelligent and articulate, the dapper Tunney quit the ring a rich man, married a wealthy heiress, became a successful businessman, and one of the most famous men in American. In 1940, in anticipation of the looming war, the Navy commissioned the former pugilist a Lieutenant Commander and installed him as the director of its Physical Training Section. Dedicated to keeping Americas' servicemen healthy and fit, Tunney was in San Francisco recruiting college athletes to serve as physical education instructors.

"I went to see the champ himself," recalled Gene. "I guess he liked what he saw because before I knew it I was on my way back to Norfolk, Virginia to start a class as a Navy physical education instructor."

THE NAVY

As a "Slick Sleeve" Chief Petty Officer. NOB Norfolk, 1942.
Crewman unidentified

XVII

***"Ya'll er shitheads.
Never volunteer for anything."***

Chief Wilson

Like a journey through the proverbial looking glass, Gene's arrival at Naval Operating Base (NOB), Norfolk, Virginia on June 10, 1942 was a passage to another world.

"It was huge," he said of the Navy's oldest and largest base. "There were thousand of guys everywhere and the base was enormous. I reported for processing. They gave us a uniform voucher of $118.00 and issued us gear. By the end of the day I was in the Navy. They assigned me to a class in the Tunney Program."

It was no Camp Comfort. In spite of the fact that most of the trainees were college athletes, the curriculum was tough and demanding - and not just physically. Along with the prescribed regimen of close order drill, calisthenics, and learning to distinguish a bulkhead from an overhead, the men were also indoctrinated in the ways of the real Navy.

"They had called this old Chief out of retirement," smiled Gene at the memory. "His name was Chief Wilson. Lord, what a character. He was a little wiry guy from the hills of Tennessee. He was tough as hell and about sixty-five years old. He trained us. Ran and marched the hell out of us. This was in the heat of the summer back there, humid as hell, and he really worked us over, showing us all the different exercises that we'd have to teach and lead."

"Anyway," he went on, "after he'd run us into the ground, he'd give us a rest. We'd all gather under a tree and he'd start in."

'Ya'll listen,' he'd drawl. 'Ya'll 'er shit heads. But I'm gonna tell ya'll about this man's Navy. First of all, never make an enemy, cause sure as hell ya'll 'er gonna have to salute the sumbitch some day! And another thing, you shit heads, and this is important. Never volunteer for anything!'

"Oh he was great," laughed Gene. "He really worked our tails off, but he also taught us the way. He was a great guy."

After ten weeks of long days and short nights, Gene's class of fifty graduated with the rank of Chief Petty Officer Specialist. It was not without controversy.

In the hierarchy of the Navy there is a well-defined schism between officers and enlisted personnel. Officers enjoy better pay, better food, better living quarters and a wider range of privileges. In the strictest sense they are in charge. But the practicality of operating a large organization, not to mention a ship, dictates a more reasonable reality. Accordingly, beyond the pomp and gold braid, smart officers recognize that the enlisted men who sail and fight their ships are indispensable. Thus, the men who held positions critical to the actual operation of the vessel wore their rank on their right arm and were held in higher esteem.

"A cook or supply guy wore his rate on the left arm," explained Gene's long time friend Jim Bligh, himself a Tunney graduate from a later class. "But the guys who held right arm rates were essential. They were the gunners, the Chief Bosons mate, the helmsmen, the motor-macs - guys you had to have to make the ship go."

"When we got out of the Tunney school," he went on, "they didn't know what to do with us so they made us Chiefs, the highest right arm rate of all."

Not un-expectantly the proud Chiefs of the old Navy, their right sleeves emblazed with crossed anchors and hash marks, justifiably held Gene and others like him in low regard, sardonically calling them as "Slick sleeves" and "Tunney Fish".

"They were pretty harsh on us," acknowledged Gene. "I couldn't blame them. It took those old-timers 25 years to make Chief and here we got the Anchors and the privileges in just a few months."

"But I didn't care. I had no intention of leading exercises stateside anyway. I wanted to get overseas. As soon as we graduated, I started looking around for a way to get out of the Tunney Program and into the action."

He didn't have far to look.

****

After witnessing the horror and futility of trench warfare in the First World War, General John A. Lejeune USMC, recognized the essential lesson of military history, namely; the dynamics of warfare constantly change and, training in the tactics of past wars was a formula for future disaster. Mobility, Lejeune realized, and the capacity to land and support troops on foreign shores were the keys to future victories.

The next day Gene's sister Milli and her husband Red were at the house for dinner. As the three of them sat on the front porch they could smell Pia's Thanksgiving meal cooking through the kitchen window. They hardly noticed the taxi as it came down Poplar Avenue and turned into the dirt driveway.

"We never got a cab at our house," said Gene. "When I saw it, I suspected what it might be. The driver had a telegram from the war department. He handed it to me and told me that Dan was missing - not dead but missing."

It was a dreadful scene. Since Giacondo and Pia could not read English, Gene translated the cryptic words on the thin paper into Italian.

Taken in Kezar Stadium on October 23, 1938, this remains one of the greatest and most poignant sports photos of all time. L to R: Dan Fisk, Bill Telesmanic, and Dante Benedetti as they celebrate a touchdown against St. Mary's.
All three of these men were lost in WWII.

"It was a very sad moment," said Gene softly. "I read it to them. And then I was very honest with them. I told them that he could be alive in a prison camp, but that he could also be dead. They didn't read English so I knew they wouldn't be able to get information. My Mother was convinced that he would come home. But in my heart I knew he was gone."

Norman Rockwell's Rosie the Riveter.

XXI

"You must tell your children, putting modesty aside,
that without us, without women
there would have been no spring in 1945."

Inscription on the Rosie the Riveter Memorial
Richmond, California.

After the holiday Gene caught the Catalina at Treasure Island for the long return flight to the east coast. As he slept to the drone of the Pratt & Whitney engines, the country that passed beneath him was experiencing a colossal awakening.

Unlike the First World War, almost all of which was fought in Europe, the Second World War was global in scope and presented enormous geographical and logistical problems. Simply put, America had to build an army and navy, train it, supply it, transport it around the world in opposite directions, and defeat a disciplined and battle tested enemy. Moreover, the Germans and Japanese were not going to lay out the welcome mat. Each port, beach, island, town and city would have to be taken under the gun before it could be liberated. No nation in the history of the world had faced a challenge so daunting.

The Axis leaders knew this. They were also banking that the citizen sons of a decadent democracy were soft and lacked the heart to fight, let alone defeat, the armies of hardened professionals they had forged in their crucibles of tyranny.

But the Axis leaders were wrong. Like Gulliver unbound, the United States had shrugged itself awake, ripped the political and social ties of complacency from their moorings, and gone to work.

The war effort affected life at every level. Putting aside political and labor issues, the nation's manufactures galvanized and became willing partners with the government. The entire automotive industry stopped producing automobiles, retooled its productions lines and began making a host of military hardware that ranged from jeeps, to B-24 bombers. And smaller corporations, like Rock-Ola Music and Underwood, stopped making juke boxes and typewriters respectively to manufacture M-1 Carbine rifles.

Along the nations seaboards, sleepy towns and villages were transformed into thriving shipbuilding centers. In the San Francisco bay area, Henry Kaiser's shipyard in Richmond (which was already making Lend Lease Liberty ships for England) expanded to triple its pre-war size. The tiny portside village of Sausalito experienced a similar metamorphosis when the Bechtel Company cleared the Richardson mud flats, pushed dirt into the bay, built buildings, recruited nearly 70,000 workers from all over America (many of them African Americans) and within a few months had Liberty Ships sliding down the ways of a new company named Marinship.

Changes were not restricted to industry. Virtually every person in the country did their part. School children collected pots and pans for scrap metal, college girls rolled bandages for the Red Cross and passed out coffee and doughnuts to boys on troop trains as they stopped in small towns across America. Gas, meat and rubber were rationed. Citizens planted victory gardens, bought war bonds and served with the Civilian Defense. Even penitentiary inmates pitched in by donating blood, buying bonds and stitching American flags. "We know what freedom really means," said one.

But perhaps the greatest change occurred in the make-up of the work force itself. With most of the men gone off to fight, manpower needs were filled by women. By the end of the war an estimated 18 million ladies had exchanged the accouterments of femininity for the coveralls, hard hats, welding torches and rivet guns of the factory worker. The advent of women in the work place necessitated the need for innovative social services. As a result, employers established day care centers for working mothers, built company housing projects like Marin City in Sausalito, and Atchison Village in Richmond and provided company sponsored health plans, (these were the first HMO's, one of which today is called Kaiser Permanente).

America's artist laureate, Norman Rockwell, painted a picture entitled Rosie the Riveter. The image depicted a tough and determined American girl dressed in overalls and welding goggles eating a ham sandwich on her lunch break, as she crushed a copy of Hitler's Mien Kampf beneath her penny loafer clad foot. Rockwell's proud and defiant Rosie became an iconic and indelible tribute to the unflagging sprit and fortitude of the gutsy women, and indeed all civilians, who fought and won the war on the home front.

"The entire country had changed almost overnight," marveled Gene at the memory. "Everyone was doing something for the war effort. We were truly a 'United States'. I knew when I saw it that somehow we would win."

CUS & EVELYN

Ensign Carmon F. Pirro USNR.
Courtesy Universtiy of Notre Dame archives.

XXII

"No matter what the future brings,
as time goes bye."

From "As Time Goes Bye"
By Herman Hupfeld

On Thursday January 28, 1943, Ensign Carmon Francis Pirro USNR, graduated from midshipmen's school. The ceremony in the new Navy Drill Hall on the campus of the University of Notre Dame, was both a testament to the resiliency of the graduates, and a reflection of the drastic manpower shortage the Navy faced as they strove to staff the hundreds of ships being built to fight the war. Known as Ninety-Day-Wonders, the newly minted Ensigns had just completed an intensive four month course and were now, for better or worse, commissioned officers and gentlemen in the United States Navy.

For Cus, the road to his commission started the previous autumn when he dropped out of law school to enlist and was ordered to report, along with thirteen hundred other men, to midshipmen's school on the fabled campus at South Bend.

It had not been easy. Classes were heavy on Spherical Trigonometry, Naval Ordinance, Seamanship, Navy Customs and endless regulations. The day started at 0600 and ended at 2200. Along with classes the men learned close order drill, did endless calisthenics, and were indoctrinated in the ways of "This Man's Navy". They swabbed the deck, cleaned the heads, (a wet sink is a dirty sink), kept an ear out for the latest scuttlebutt, sacked out at taps, and learned to distinguish a chock from a bit, a fantail from a foc'sle and a barnacle from a binnacle.

Each day a man was designated "Mate of the Deck" and was responsible for seeing that "The Word" was passed to the rest of the men in his room. Woe be unto he who missed the word. And damn the punster who ran the passageway shouting "All who have not done so, do so immediately." The relentless pace along with constant exams, inspections of rooms and uniforms, and unrelenting military discipline, wore many down. Over two hundred washed out after the first month.

The survivors were advanced from apprentice Seaman to Midshipmen. Now attired in the raiment of a naval officer instead of the traditional "middie" uniform of bell bottom trousers, flap blouse and blue ringed Dixie cup cap, the pace intensified. The men studied Navigation, Damage Control and the Watch Officers Guide and Manual. Off-hours were spent washing uniforms, studying, or playing pick-up basketball in the Rockne Memorial Gym.

On one of the few weekends that Cus had liberty, Evelyn came for a visit and the two attended a football game. Sitting together in the excitement of the "house that Rockne built", they watched legendary coach Frank Leahy's men defeat the Wildcats from Northwestern University. The experience made Evelyn a lifetime fan of the Irish. And now as Cus listened to the speaker exhort he and his classmates to "Come home with your shields of honor untarnished, or come home on them," he surely must have reflected on his future, and the joy and uncertainty of it all.

The couple had enjoyed a wonderful courtship. Cus had taken Evelyn home to his parents where she was warmly welcomed to their hill-top home in Solvay.

"That old house was wonderful," remembered Cus's niece, Rockette. "It was two stories and everyone always entered by the side door and went down to the big basement. There was a big table and kitchen down there where Grandma Marian did all of her cooking. Grandpa Thomas – who everyone called "The Chief" - also made his wine down there. It was all very Italian. And the place was always alive with people and friends and lots of food and fellowship."

Likewise, in visits that were warm and sometimes humorous, Evelyn had taken Cus home to meet her family. On one occasion he brought along brother Rocco and several of his strapping football pals to supper. After the meal, at her father Gordon's urging, Evelyn's mother Marian gathered the boys around the piano for an after supper sing. More than sixty years later Rocco's wife, Ida, told the story. "To get those football jocks to sing was like casting pearl before swine", she laughed. "Cus had a nice voice, but Rock couldn't carry a tune to save his soul. None of those guys could. They were clods. But Cus growled, 'All right you guys shut up and sing!' And I guess they tried. It must have sounded awful. Poor Mrs. Birrel, poor Evelyn!"

Evelyn's sister Bobbi laughed when reminded of the evening. "Actually," she chuckled, "Cus had a very nice voice. But the other boys … well I just don't know."

But the couple also dealt with some serious issues – specifically a difference of religion.

"In those days," explained Evelyn, "religion was a major difference in society. The rules of the church were much stricter. Cus and I talked about it a great deal when we started dating. I gave it a lot of thought. Converting to Catholicism made sense to me. After all, it was the first church – all the others came after. I loved Cus and he loved me. We felt like that from the very first. I wanted to be with him, and in his church. I decided to convert and become a Catholic."

It was not a choice lightly taken.

"Joining the church was and is a serious decision," noted Father Michael Kotlanger S.J. "A person seeking to become a Catholic in the 1940s would first approach a priest and express their interest. A program of scheduled meetings and assigned readings would be established. In those days, readings would have centered on the Baltimore Catechism Book, a common textbook that taught our faith. Usually, after a year of instruction, the convert would be received into the church community in a formal baptism ceremony."

Evelyn on left, and her best friend Betty O'Brian-Bligh.

"I went to the monastery down the street from Catholic University," said Evelyn. "I talked to the priest who gave me all the readings. I must admit that I didn't read them thoroughly. But the Father knew my heart. Finally, even though I'd not done all the reading, he approved my conversion and I was baptized. Cus and I decided to get married when he finished Midshipmen's school."

And so it was on January 31, 1943, three days after the graduation at Notre Dame, that Cus and Evelyn were married at St. Johns Catholic Church in Forest Glenn, Maryland. It was a wartime wedding.

"I remember that Cus was trying to find enough guys to be in the wedding party," said Joe Ratigan, his old roommate from Law School. "He had left a message for me, but by that time I was in South America on an intelligence assignment with the Navy."

But Cus's younger sister Rose was there. And Betty O'Brien, Evelyn's lifelong friend who had baptized her as a child in the bath tub, was there to serve as maid of honor. Betty's fiancé Jim Bligh remembers: "It was a small wedding, but very beautiful. They were a stunning couple really. They were very much in love."

OPERATION HUSKY
THE INVASION OF SICILY

Gene and Jim Bligh seeing the sights in Algiers, 1943

XXIII

"You are going to meet the Boche.
Carve your name in his face!"

General Lucien L. Truscott, USA
on the eve of the Sicilian invasion.

By the beginning of 1943 America was fighting back. On the home front, the country had mobilized and the nation's vast military and industrial machine was in high gear. The previous May in the Pacific, the US Navy had fought the Japanese to a standstill in the battle of the Coral Sea. One month later, on June 4, 1942, they soundly thrashed the Imperial Fleet in a stunning victory at Midway. In the British Solomons, after a bloody six month campaign, US Marines were on the verge of defeating the Japanese at Guadalcanal. In North Africa, Allied forces had scored their first victory with operation TORCH and secured French Morocco and Algeria. Meanwhile in Europe, after sweeping successes the previous year, Hitler's drive into Russia had stalled at Stalingrad.

Thus in the glow of these successes, on January 14, 1943, President Franklin Roosevelt (who loved adventure) became the first president to fly while in office – and the first to visit troops in the field since Abraham Lincoln when he traveled to the Moroccan city of Casablanca to meet Prime Minister Winston Churchill. In an historic conference, the two diplomats turned warlords sat in the bougainvillea shaded gardens of the Hotel Anfa to decide the course of the war, and by extension, the fate of thousands of young men like Gene Benedetti and Carmon Pirro who were destined to fight it.

There was much to discuss. German submarines were wrecking havoc in the Atlantic and would have to be dealt with. The United States had gained the initiative in the Pacific, and did not want to relinquish it. Russian leader Josef Stalin, whose gallant forces were taking horrific losses while engaging upwards of 185 German divisions, was haranguing the Allies for relief in the form of a second front. And most important, a decision had to be made as to when Allied forces would cross the English Channel and fight the German army.

For their part, the Americans wanted to leave a token force in North Africa, use England as a base to build up their forces, and launch a cross-channel attack that summer. But early reverses had made the English reluctant to assume such a risk. They proposed an invasion of the Italian mainland through Sicily. Such an operation, they argued, would give the Allies access to what Churchill called the "soft underbelly of Europe", while knocking Italy out of the war and diverting German resources from the Russian front. The two sides argued vehemently. The British won. When the conference was adjourned nine days later, the parties agreed that the Allies would accept nothing less than unconditional surrender. A cross-channel invasion would be postponed until after 1943. Priority would be given to the submarine problem. The United States would maintain its initiative in the Pacific. And Stalin would get his second front. Sicily would be taken as a prelude to invading Italy.

****

On the afternoon of July 8, 1943, Gene Benedetti stood in the pilot house of LCT-443 as it plowed through the waters of the Mediterranean Sea. The sky was clear and the sea was calm. Bound for the coast of Sicily, It seemed like nothing could stop the hundreds of haze-gray warships that steamed all around him. But that night the sunset was blood red. And the following morning brought a low and misty dawn. Savvy sailors knew the signs and braced themselves. The mythic Gods of the Mediterranean were about to bring their wrath. The storm that followed "... was one of those mistrals that have bedeviled sailormen in the Mediterranean since the dawn of history," wrote Samuel Eliot Morison of the gale. "It was just such a one that Poseidon raised on the 'wine-dark sea' to pester Menelaus, or that wrecked St. Paul on the coast of Malta." Indeed, with winds blowing up to force 7 the situation aboard Gene's LCT (loaded down with three tanks and sixty combat troops) became desperate. The men were drenched as solid seas crashed over the gunnels and battered them into a miserable seasickness. Up on the bridge, Gene struggled to keep the flat bottomed craft positioned and afloat.

"It was very frightening," he said. "It blew like hell. It was worse than the hurricane back home and there was no place to tie up. I thought we would all go down. I couldn't believe the Mediterranean could be that rough."

Known to the Romans as Mare Nostrum, (our sea) there is perhaps no body of water richer in history than the Mediterranean

Sea. Bound on the west by the Straits of Gibraltar and on the east by the Suez Canal, the almost land-locked Med is the inland sea of Europe, Asia, and Africa. In Greek mythology King Poseidon, the son of the Titans and the brother of Zeus, ruled from its depths. In centuries past its ports embarked the wooden fleets of antiquity. And now, in the spring of 1943, the cycle of history had once again brought a great armada of warships to its ancient waters.

Gene and his crew had arrived in early April. By this time he had been promoted to Ensign. "LCT's were commissioned ships," he explained. "Since only an officer could command a ship they gave us all spot commissions before we left the states. It didn't change much. I'd been driving my ship, since I'd picked her up in Philly and I'd also been helping to train other skippers. But the promotions put us in compliance with regulations."

"The trip over was really something," he continued. "They took us across on a big LST. They sat our ships on chocks on the deck and lashed them down. When we got to the Med, they flooded the LST to one side until it listed over on its beam at about 45 degrees. LCT's were very buoyant. The whole underside of them was actually open tanks that could be flooded when you needed to ballast them down. So, when they knocked the chocks out, and our ship slid over the side, it floated like a cork. It was very interesting to watch and very efficient. After they slid our ship in the water, we went aboard with all our stuff. We were ready to go. We were in the war."

At the time of Gene's arrival the Germans were on the run. Unable to exploit his advances over the Americans at Kasserine Pass a few months earlier, German Field Marshall Erwin Rommel, the legendary Desert Fox, had been recalled. By the first of May over 240,000 German prisoners had fallen under allied control.

"When we got there our first action was an end run to Oran in Algeria," said Gene. "There wasn't much to it. It was mostly supply and support. But we were still bombed every day from the air. That was awful. We were bombed from the day we got to the Med until the day we left. You just got used to it. By the middle of May the Krauts had been run out of Bizerte and we moved in."

Situated on the northeast coast of Tunisia a few miles northwest of the ancient city of Carthage, Bizerte had been a vital strategic base and point of embarkation to the Mediterranean for centuries. Established by the Phoenicians around 1000 B.C. it was originally called Hippo Diarrhytus. It is connected by canal to two inner harbors, the bay of Scbra, and the Lake of Bizerte.

"The damage when we got there was awful," recalled Gene. "The harbor was really beat up. There were blown up ships and all kinds of debris in the channels. But our salvage guys and engineers cleared it all away and we set up a huge base. We started getting ready for Sicily."

Sicily, the Mediterranean's largest island, sits at the tip of the Italian boot as if kicked by Italy into the sea. Its southern shore lies a mere ninety miles from the coast of North Africa, while its northern tip nearly touches the mainland at the narrow straits of Messina. It has been a target of conquest for centuries. For the Allies, taking Sicily was crucial if they were to gain control of the sea lanes between their African bases and the Italian peninsula. The enemy knew this, and garrisoned the island with ten Italian and three German divisions.

The overall invasion plan called for a combined force of British and Americans to embark from the coast of North Africa, cross the Mediterranean, land troops, tanks and supplies on Sicily's southern shores and fight their way inland. Supported by air and naval gunfire, General George S. Patton's 7th Army was tasked to land on the left flank, while British General Bernard Montgomery's 8th Army would land on the right. Together the combined forces would occupy a front that covered nearly the entire islands southern coast.

The Americans were organized into three major attack forces. From west to east they were coded named JOSS, DIME and CENT. Gene's flotilla was assigned to JOSS force. Their mission was to transport the tanks and men of the 3rd Infantry Division commanded by General Lucien L. Truscott (USA) and two Ranger battalions to the beaches adjacent to the small coastal town of Licata, which represented the farthest point west on the allied line of attack. D-day was scheduled for Saturday July 10, 1943.

At the time, HUSKY was the largest amphibious operation in recorded history. The logistics required to execute such an undertaking were enormous. For days prior to the invasion the roads and waters in and around Bizerte were clogged as thousands of men and tons of equipment converged on the harbor to board the hundreds of waiting invasion ships. The air swirled with the sounds and smells of smoking machinery, shouting men, and clouds of brown dust, all swept by the blistering Sirocco's that blew in off the North African desert. To add to the confusion, German air raids bombed the harbor on a regular basis, sending men scurrying for shelter and gunners to their battle stations.

"The activity was just unbelievable," recalled Gene. "We took on a load of tanks and about 60 combat engineers. After we were loaded, we took off into the Med to rendezvous."

With the three American attack groups embarking from different ports, the task of bringing them together safely in the middle of the ocean was daunting. To solve the problem, Allied mine sweepers cleared a ten mile wide strait dubbed the Tunisian War Channel. Thus protected from mines and submarines the convoys had clear sailing to a seagoing "marshalling yard" seven miles west of Gozo Island near Malta, where they would be organized into assault waves.

Things were going perfectly when the storm hit and hurled the plan into such disarray that allied commanders seriously considered aborting the invasion.

"That storm clobbered us," said Gene grimly. "But our training really paid off. We had no choice. We just hung in there and applied what we'd learned. But I'll tell you, it was tough. That damn LCT was like trying to steer a lead weight. I still don't know how we managed to maneuver into formation and head out for Sicily."

But maneuver they did, and as the storm battered day turned to night, the crossing proved to be the first of several brushes with history for Gene.

"Going over, the storm was hitting us so hard that I had a hell of a time staying on course," he recalled. "My little compass was not reliable in those conditions. It was so dark that we had trouble seeing the other ships. It was almost impossible. From time to time, I'd spot a break in the clouds and try to find the North Star. It was my only way to navigate."

"Anyway, the commanding officer of the men I was carrying – a Lt. Colonel - came up to the bridge and asked if he could help. I told him I was trying to keep my bearing on the North Star. He took up a look-out post on the deck outside the pilot house. He had a sharp eye and was a great help. We got to talking and as it turned out he was General Hap Arnold's son!"

One of America's early aviation pioneers, Henry H. "Hap" Arnold learned to fly from the Wright brothers. By the time Gene met his son Hank, Arnold was the Commanding General of the Army Air Corps, and eventually would retire as a five-star General.

Roosevelt and Chruchill at Casablanca - two diplomats turned warlord.

"Hank was really a down to earth guy," said Gene. "When I offered to make accommodations for him in our quarters he refused and said he'd rather sleep with his troops. As we talked, he found out that I was from Sonoma County. He told me his dad had just purchased land there and was going to live there after the war. We exchanged addresses and promised to look each other up when we got back. He was really a nice guy. Very humble – very unpretentious."

Force JOSS was divided into four attack groups; Gaffi, Molla, Salso and Falconara. Under the command of Captain Lorenzo S. Sabin (USN), Attack Group Gaffi was comprised of 7 LST's, 17 LCI's and Gene's flotilla of 21 LCT's. Their mission was to land the 7th Regimental Combat Team approximately 1000 yards west of Licata. It would be a vatic repeat of history. For it was in this same area that the Roman armies of Regulus and Marcellus had landed to fight the Carthaginians in the Punic Wars. Now, over two thousand years later, legionnaires with gladius and lance were replaced by American boys with M1's and K-bars, slowly coming ashore on this stormy summer night to fight on the historic beaches of Sicily.

As Attack Group Gaffi approached the leeward side of the island the fierce storm began to moderate.

General George Patton.
"He looked like he's stepped out of a haberdashery."

"We got into position about 10:30 pm that night," remembered Gene. "The storm had been awful, and we were so glad that it had let up. The sky cleared up and we could see the stars. No one knew what to expect. It was our first real action."

By 1:30 am group Gaffi's troop laden LCI's were plowing through the still heavy seas toward the beach. With the skies now clear, enemy dive bombers, (which had attacked the convoy before it anchored), intensified, and the dark sky was soon filled with tracers as every ship afloat fired their guns at the sound of the motors. It was terrifying, bobbing in the dark seas like blind ducks hoping not to get hit. Group leader Captain Sabin had the experience of feeling his LCI literally lift out of the water when a bomb exploded nearby. Ashore, enemy lookouts, having discounted the possibility of an attack in such violent weather, were caught off guard. As a result, the five Italian divisions and 34,000 Germans that were available to defend Licata responded poorly, with only a portion of them putting up a stout fight. For a while, though, it was enough.

"We could see the muzzle flashes ashore," said Gene. "that and the air raids were very disconcerting to say the least."

By 2:45 am the LCI's, under heavy small arms fire, were spilling the first waves of troops on the beach. Among them were the men of the 7th Infantry Regiment. Known as the "Cotton Balers", (a proud sobriquet acquired in the war of 1812 when their predecessors fought the British from behind stacked bales of

"The Germans bombed us every day.."
A cargo ship explodes and sinks in Sicily.

cotton in the battle of New Orleans), they were the 2nd oldest regiment in the US Army. Now cured of their seasickness, they lived up to their motto; Volens et Potens (willing and able) as they tore "like a pack of hounds" into the enemy. Like all ground troops that morning they landed in "light order" wearing olive woolen shirts, twill pants tucked into high leggings, netted helmets and carrying only their weapons, ammunition, and field packs. Time was of the essence in supporting them with heavy armor and tanks. Toward that end, their commanding officer, General Lucien Truscott, was desperate for his tanks to come ashore. Thus, in spite of the hot action on the beach, all LCT's were ordered to "charge the beach" and land their tanks. With the Navy's destroyers blasting away at enemy shore installations, this was done in the bravest of fashion.

"We went in and got our tanks and men off," recalled Gene. "It was hot. We were taking fire, but we managed."

By 11:00 am all units had achieved their objectives and Licata was captured. At this point Gene's role changed from that of an attacker to that of a ferryman, transporting food, ammunition, medical supplies and other matériel needed to reinforce the troops ashore. As the day progressed he was ordered to take a load of steel girders into the small man-made harbor at Licata where engineers were building a ramp. It was here that he saw for the first time the human suffering wrought by war and tyranny.

"My ship was the first one into the harbor," he said. "I'll never forget it. The town was all torn up. I pulled my ship right up to the shore. The village priest with about twenty of his parishioners came down to the waters edge. He was dressed in a shabby robe and his flock looked worse, ragged clothes, haggard faces, all scared and hungry."

"I came down off the bridge, and walked up to the bow. I could look right down at the priest. I called out in Italian; 'Padre, cosa visi besonia? (Father, what do you need?). His whole face lit up. He couldn't believe that I spoke Italian. He told me his people needed everything, especially clothing. I ordered my men to take all of their extra clothes, underwear, socks, that kind of thing and give them to him. They had nothing. The Germans had taken everything. We gave them all we had. I knew I could get my men more stuff from supply. I gave them what we had, and later brought a bunch more to them. I felt so sorry for them. The war was so hard on them. The experience really woke me up."

Ships like Gene's carried everything but the kitchen sink.

Throughout the day the LCT's continued to deliver all manner of matériel onto the beaches off the Liberty and transport ships that were anchored offshore. To the east of Licata, in an area called the Gela plain, a contingent of General George S. Patton's tanks had landed and driven to the hills beyond the beaches where they were halted by a group of German panzers. As the tanks sat on the hillside exchanging fire, Gene received a message.

"I got a semaphore message (we were under radio silence) and was ordered to go to the flag ship," he said. "When we got there an army sergeant came climbing down the net. He said he was on General Patton's staff and wanted to know if I could land

Patton on the beach and keep him dry. I told them that I could get him close, but that he was going to get wet because I couldn't get my ship right up on the shore. He said he'd arrange for a pontoon to be floated out and climbed back up the ropes."

Moments later, in another brush with history, Gene watched the colorful General and his staff climb down the side of the USS Monrovia and step into his ship.

"He looked like he had stepped out of a haberdashery," chuckled Gene. "He had on his riding boots, his helmet with the stars, his riding crop, and of course his ivory handled pistols. I'll tell you, he was a sight to behold!"

"We spoke a few words," he went on. "I asked him if he could take care of the Germans. He said he didn't know about the Germans but that his men 'sure as hell wouldn't be sitting still for long.'"

"We could see his tanks up on the hills engaged with some German panzers. They had been pinned down for several hours. The Sergeant told me to wait a few minutes after they got ashore and 'the General will have those damn tanks on the move.'"

"When we got to the beach," he continued, "they had a jeep waiting, and floated a pontoon out for him. I kept my field glasses on the tanks up in the hills and sure enough, about fifteen minutes later they were on the move and driving the Germans back. I guess those tankers were more afraid of Patton than they were the krauts!"

The conquest of Sicily took thirty-eight bloody days and cost the allies over 30,000 causalities. During the entire time Gene and his crew ferried supplies and men between Bizerte and Sicily. It was grueling duty. The men worked from sunup to sunset. They slept in the cramped hot quarters and ate in the tiny galley or on the pitching deck. Constantly plagued by fatigue and never ending air raids, their days were long, difficult and dangerous. As a result, they developed a unique esprit de corps.

"It was a dangerous job," said Gene quietly. "We all became very close. We were like a family. It was ironic though. With all that was going on, the air raids and that kind of stuff, I was never afraid to die. It was happening all around me. It just became an accepted part of life. That and my faith kept me going."

"A couple of my men were Irish Catholics from Boston," he explained, "Every morning we'd sit down for a few minutes. We'd read a few verses from the Bible and say a prayer. I never insisted that anyone attend these meetings. In fact I never said much about them at all. Many of the kids in my crew – and they were kids, most of them just 18 and 19 years old - were from the south and were Baptists. And a few of them had no religion of any kind. Of course, I was a Catholic. Anyway, over time our meetings grew to include the entire crew - even the kids with no religion. We just met for a moment each morning, read a verse or two and asked God to bless and keep us through the day. There was no distinction between our churches. We figured that God scored us all the same."

On several occasions they transported prisoners, an experience that affected Gene in different ways.

"We transported a load of Italian prisoners," he laughed. "We picked them up and they were overjoyed to be aboard. They didn't want to fight. Since I spoke Italian, I talked to them. We had a ball. They sunbathed on the deck. We sang songs together. We had a great time. They just wanted the war to be over so they could go home. They truly felt as if they had been liberated."

The Germans, however, were a different story.

"We brought some of those guys back too. They were unbelievable. They stood on deck in ranks at attention in the hot sun for the entire crossing. I talked to their commanding officer and told him to sit his men down and relax, that it was a long crossing. But he would have none of it. He was very arrogant. I didn't like him. When he told me that their defeat was 'just a temporary setback,' and that they were going to win because they were the 'master race' I knew that we were in for a long war."

But it wasn't all work. Between invasions there was ample time for the men to enjoy liberty as well as less traditional pursuits. World War II LCT flotillas were comprised of the smallest commissioned ships in the Navy. Manned primarily by draftees, and commanded almost entirely by reservists who acted more like coaches than naval officers, their maintenance and supply needs ranked at the bottom of fleet schedules. Consequently, the young LCT'ers often had to fend for themselves to acquire parts, supplies and other niceties that were more readily available to sailors on larger vessels. The result was a swashbuckling band of blue jackets who behaved more like Corsairs of the Barbary Coast than sailors in the US Navy. For Gene it was a natural fit.

"I became quite a horse trader," he grinned. "We'd unload all kinds of stores from our Liberty ships and also from the British ships. Personally I found the Limeys to be very civilized. Every day they'd stop at 10:00 in the morning and at 3:00 in the afternoon and have a drink! They called it 'splicing the main brace'. The officers got scotch and the enlisted men got a jigger of Lord Nelson's Rum. The scotch came twelve bottles to a case, but the rum came in two gallon jugs. That stuff was rough too. Like syrup - one hundred and ninety proof. You couldn't drink it straight – it would kill you. They would dilute it with warm water."

Never one to shun civility and forever in search of cultural enrichment, Gene quickly adopted the British tradition.

"We lived high on the hog," he grinned. "We'd unload that stuff and I'd always keep a case or two of scotch and some jugs of rum. I'd use it as trade bait. We could get cigars and cigarettes from the American ships and booze from the British. I'd trade that stuff for food and ice cream - especially ice cream. The men loved it. We'd trade it for all kinds of stuff, vegetables, fresh fruit, you name it. We were like pirates!"

"We had a lot of time between invasions," he continued. "One time I decided that we needed some transportation to get around Bizerte. There was a huge area where all of the captured equipment was stored. They had everything, trucks, cars, motorcycles, hundreds of them. So anyway, I went down there in a jeep. An Army Sergeant was standing guard and says to me, 'What can I do for you, skipper?' I told him I'd like to get a car. 'Take your pick,' he says. So I started looking and found a beautiful Fiat limousine. It was an Italian General's car. It was black with a spare tire on each side and a window between the driver and the back seat. It even had the little flag holders on the front fenders with the General's flags still in them. It was beautiful! The Sergeant traded the car and a big BMW four cylinder motorcycle for two pillows! I couldn't believe it! He even filled them with gas for me! I took the car and motorcycle back and we kept them on the ship when we were in port so we could get around town."

"Later," he went on, "I talked a skipper of a merchant ship that I grown friendly with to take the car to New York on his next stateside run. I wrote my brother-in-law, Red Libarle, and told him to expect a telegram from the skipper when they got to New York. Red was going to make arrangements to ship the car to

California and give it to my dad. He would have just loved that car! But the ship was sunk on the way home and I never heard from the captain again."

The base also offered other distractions.

"They had built a couple of big hospitals behind Bizerte," Gene explained. "They brought all the wounded there. Of course they were staffed with nurses. We'd go to dances at the officer's club and dance with the nurses or take them out on the town."

"We also got to travel," he went on. "I got to see the old city of Carthage, and all the ruins in the area. I went to Algiers and saw the sights with my friend Jim Bligh. It was really something. I had a great time."

To counter the inherent boredom of garrison life the allies also built recreation centers. Ever the athlete, Gene regularly took advantage of these facilities, playing basketball, volleyball and softball with other soldiers and sailors. One day while working out, he met a tall Italian kid from upstate New York. His name was Carmon Pirro and the two quickly struck up a warm friendship.

"Cus was such a nice guy," smiled Gene at the memory. "We met at the gym. We had so much in common. We were friends from the moment we met."

CUS PIRRO
AND
THE SCOUTS & RAIDERS

Scouts & Raiders emblem.

XXIV

"Cus Pirro was definitely the kind of guy they were looking for."

J. Barry Dwyer

In late February 1943, after a two week honeymoon with Evelyn, Cus Pirro reported to the Navy's Amphibious Training Base (ATB) at Little Creek, Virginia. A primary training center for amphibious warfare, the sprawling facility was also the original home to a special force that was virtually unknown. They were called the Scouts and Raiders (S&R) and were the first of their kind in American history. Formed in the summer of 1942, this top secret unit drew its initial all volunteer roster from the ranks of Chief Specialists in the Tunney Program and from the nearby Solomon Island Boat Training Program. The original ten Tunney Fish in the group were especially notable and set the standard for future generations of elite fighters. All were college graduates and stood six feet or better. All were athletes and had played college ball. And some had played in the professional ranks. First tested in combat in Operation Torch, where they reconnoitered enemy beaches and installations and guided assault waves onto invasion beaches, they had earned an astonishing eight Navy Crosses for valor under fire. For over fifty years their exploits lay hidden from history. But in 1992, author, historian and patriot, John B. Dwyer published a seminal tribute to these gallant men. Dwyer's book, entitled *Scouts & Raiders*, brought to light for the first time what only a few had known for years; that within the soul of every modern day Navy SEAL beat the heart of America's first warrior's elite - the brave and indefatigable Scouts and Raiders.

"A man like Cus Pirro fit the S&R profile perfectly," declared Dwyer in a 2003 interview. "He was big, tough, well educated, athletic, clever, intelligent and disciplined. He put to rest the myth of the dumb jock. He was definitely the kind of guy they were looking for."

By the time Cus volunteered, the S&R's primary school had moved from Little Creek to Ft. Pierce, Florida. But after their contribution in the Sicilian campaign, they had established an advanced training base in Bizerte. Records are sketchy, and it is not known precisely when Cus arrived in theater. But by all accounts it was in Bizerte that he received most of his specialized training.

"Everything the S&R's did," explained Dwyer, "was at the very least classified Secret and most of it was classified Top Secret. Their activities were shrouded in mystery. They traveled under secret orders in small groups one or two guys at a time, and met up with their unit at their destination. Only they and their commanders knew who or what they were. For the most part, there were no records kept. Since there is no memory of his being in Florida, it's probable that Pirro took his basic amphibious training at Little Creek and his S&R training overseas."

Dwyer's conclusion fits with Evelyn's recollection. "Cus was never in Florida," she said. "He was always in Virginia and would sneak off base to come home at night and on weekends.

"I never knew much about what he was doing," she went on. "But when he shipped out, I was pregnant. Having him leave was heartbreaking. Neither of us wanted him to go."

S&R training was fierce. It had to be. After Operation JUBLIEE (a disastrous Canadian/British raid on the French coastal town of Dieppe in August of 1942) allied planners had climbed a steep learning curve in the still evolving art of amphibious warfare. Hence, when Operation TORCH was launched three months later, the acquisition of reliable pre-invasion intelligence was seen as vital. As one old Marine put it, "If you're going to land a bunch of 32-ton Sherman tanks on the beach you'd better make damn sure that they won't sink in the sand."

The Scouts and Raiders were mulit-talended. Here a pontoon from a French seaplane is converted into a scout boat. The man at the wheel is L.L. Culver, Cus's comanding officer.
Courtesy Naval UDT museum Ft. Pierce, FL.

The primary mission of S&R units was stealthy reconnaissance. They were the first visitors to an invasion beach, usually weeks before the actual attack. Their work required nerves of steel, iron discipline and arduous training. Over an approximately two month period Cus became an expert in the arts of reconnaissance. He learned to pilot, navigate, and repair custom crafts like the 36' scout boat, the folboat (a collapsible two man boat) and the two man kayak. Gunnery courses gave him a working knowledge of the .50 caliber machine gun, the .30 caliber Browning

Automatic Rifle (BAR), the .45 caliber Thompson submachine gun and the .38 and .45 caliber automatic pistol. Radio classes included both voice and code. In signal courses he learned semaphore, signal flags, damage control lights and Beach Marking Lamps.

There was a heavy emphasis on hand to hand combat and silent killing. Cus learned how to kill with the knife, club, and garrote. He also learned the 13 pressure points on the body so if necessary, he could kill an enemy with his bare hands. Physical training included swimming, speed marching, endless running in the sand, and a tough obstacle course. He learned the art of "sneak and peek", how to analyze and record beach gradients, take soil samples, chart tidal patterns and identify silhouetted landmarks. In short, he mastered the myriad skills required to thoroughly gather, record, and analyze all pertinent information of a targeted beach. By the time he was done, Cus Pirro was a professionally trained killer and reconnaissance expert – truly a warrior who "owned the night."

Two S&R's in a kayak.
Courtesy Naval UDT Museum
Ft. Pierde, FL.

SALERNO
OPERATION AVALANCHE

The Temple of Neptune at Paestum.

XXV

". . . Sweet the memory is to me
Of a land beyond the sea . . ."
From Amalfi by Henry Wadsworth Longfellow

At 1:20 am on the morning of September 9, 1943 the anchor chain of LST–314 broke the night silence as it rattled through the hawse pipe and splashed into the water eight miles off the coast of Salerno, Italy. Moments later a crew of blue jackets quietly lowered a 36 foot scout boat from the davits and watched six men climb aboard. With the muffled motors thrumming quietly the boat pushed off from the looming transport, turned toward the dark shoreline, and carried Carmon Pirro into combat.

Cus's voyage had started the previous May when President Roosevelt and Prime Minister Churchill convened the Trident Conference in Washington D.C. The primary question at Trident was what to do after Sicily was captured. "Would Sicily," asked Churchill, "prove to be to be a sofa or a springboard?" As at Casablanca four months earlier, the two sides held divergent views. The Americans wanted to focus on invading France while the British sought an extended campaign in Italy. Once again, the two sides argued, this time more respectfully, and again the British won. Italy would be invaded. The only question was when and where.

By late summer planners had settled on the Bay of Salerno. Despite the fact that it could be covered by the Germans from the high ground, its long beaches were suitable for landing and it was within range of Sicily based fighter squadrons. Moreover, planners felt the pending Italian surrender (Mussolini had fallen from power and secret surrender talks were underway) would further deplete enemy resistance. The operation was code named AVALANCHE. D-day was set for September 9, 1943. Pre-invasion reconnaissance was assigned to the same Scouts and Raiders that were used in HUSKY.

While all this was going on Cus was living with his fellow S&R's in their quarters at the Villa Camille in Bizerte. With a six foot shell hole in the wall and a balcony overlooking the lake, the two-story former French officers club was considered a prime billet. In between air raids, Cus continued to train, pull maintenance duty, and tour the sights. He also found time to play basketball and softball with Gene and the guys at the gym, and exchange letters with Evelyn, who by now was seven months pregnant with their first child. It was during this time that he had his own brush with history.

Lt. (j.g.) Phil Bucklew was a six-foot two-inch former professional football player from Columbus, Ohio. An original S&R from the first class at Little Creek, the charismatic ex-fullback had already won a Navy Cross for his heroics in Operation TORCH. After the war Bucklew became a career officer. By the time he retired, he was the acknowledged "Father of Naval Special Warfare". Today the Phil H. Bucklew Center for US Navy Special Warfare in Coronado, California memorializes his service. For the

Salerno operation Bucklew selected Cus to command his scout boat.

Situated south of Naples on the west coast of Italy, the scenic Gulf of Salerno runs roughly north to south for a distance of about thirty miles. At the southern tip of the bay sat the small town of Agropoli, at the northern end, the charming little city of Salerno. Inland from the crescent shaped beaches a plain cultivated with crops, dairy farms and groves rose in a gentle slope to the foothills and mountains beyond. The plan called for British forces to land on the northern rim and take Salerno. The Americans were to come ashore eight miles south opposite the ancient city of Paestum. In antiquity Paestum had been the Greek city of Poseidonia. Its citizens rich in culture, its gardens fragrant with roses, its streets and life centered on its magnificent temples, whose classic columns still stood vigil on the plain. Two man S&R teams were assigned to reconnoiter the four invasion beaches code-named from left to right, Red, Green, Yellow and Blue.

On the afternoon of September 5th, the various convoys for AVALANCHE embarked from their respective ports of Oran, Tripoli and Algiers. The next day a large LST convoy, after laying a huge smoke screen to thwart a 180 plane air raid, sortied from Bizerte. As in the Sicilian invasion, the enormous fleet organized itself en route (this time off the coast of Sicily) and set out for the Italian mainland. Aboard LST-314 Cus and his veteran crew, Larry L'Heureux, and seamen Martin and Leonard, checked and rechecked their equipment. Their job was to embark Lt. Bucklew and Ens. Ray King to a spot approximately a half mile off shore from Red beach and launch them in a two man kayak.

As the massive convoy plowed through the dark seas it was announced that Italy had surrendered. The news brought a mixed reaction, causing the assault troops to relax while prompting their officers to warn that the Germans were now their primary foe and were certainly awaiting their arrival. By 1:00 am on the morning of the 9th, the fleet had arrived off Salerno.

After pushing off from the LST, and making two stops to rendezvous with reference vessels, Cus hove too a half mile from the beach and prepared to launch Bucklew and King. Just then a burst of shell fire illuminated the coast allowing them to see the shore and identify landmarks. The two men slipped into the tiny kayak and began paddling shoreward. When they got within fifty feet of the beach they turned south and proceeded along the shore line, verifying beaches and signaling seaward as they went. With the beaches now identified, scout boats commanded by other S&R's could anchor in the proper places and guide the assault waves to their assigned beaches by flashing colored signal lights. It was a harrowing night for all hands. When the shooting started, Bucklew and King were so close to shell and rocket fire that they actually had to brush burning ashes from their clothing. In another salvo Bucklew's belt buckle was blown off. But the mission was completed and the two S&R's made it back safely. It was Cus' first taste of action and like all S&R's that night, he preformed brilliantly.

Ashore at Paestum the sun rose at 3:30 am and, as it had for over two thousand years, filtered through the Doric columns of the temple of Neptune and awakened the sleeping deities within. Had the Gods looked to the sea they would have seen hundreds of incoming assault craft laden with American boys churning through the blue water and landing on the white sand. Had they glanced to the hills, they would have seen the German Tenth Army waiting to shoot them down.

Gene arrived at the end of the first day. "We got there toward late afternoon," he recalled. "By that time, except for the air raids, things had quieted down a bit. But my God, that was a bloody beach. I'll tell you, that was a bloody beach."

The landings at Salerno were some of the most fiercely contested in World War II. Thanks to the discipline and leadership of the officers, the indescribable courage of the young soldiers, the pin-point accuracy of naval gunfire support ships (that stood off shore and blasted the Germans without mercy) and the brave sailors like Gene and his men who ferried matériel to the beaches amid the unrelenting air raids, the battle was won. Finally on September 25, 1943, the Gulf of Salerno – Longfellow's "land beyond the sea" was declared secure.

CUS IS LOST

Taken at Advanced Amphibious Base Bizerte. L to R: Ens. Jerry Donnell, Cus Pirro, Ken Howe, courtesy L.L. Culver and J. Barry Dwyer.

XXVI

"Where have all the soldiers gone?
Gone to graveyards everyone;
When will they ever learn?"

From Where Have All the Flowers Gone?
by Pete Seeger

Following the hard fought landings at Salerno and the subsequent capture of Naples, the Allies had begun fighting their way up the Italian boot toward Rome. The Germans, under Field Marshall Albert Kesselring, fought a tough and orderly withdrawal that slowly drew the invaders north. In mid-November they turned and held with a string of interlocking defensive positions called the Winter Line.

To break the impasse it was decided to attack the Germans right flank from the sea, hook up with forces fighting up the peninsula and drive the Nazis north. The old Roman resort town of Anzio was selected as the invasion site. The operation was coded named SHINGLE. D-day was set for January 22, 1944. As with Sicily and Salerno detailed pre-invasion reconnaissance was needed. Thus in late December, S&R's Cus Pirro, Ken Howe and Jerry Donnell were summoned to the headquarters of CIC RDAM

Frank J. Lowry at a Versailles-like former king's palace in Caserta, north of Naples. The Allied plans called for a reconnaissance mission to survey and evaluate the landing beaches at Anzio. It was not the first such mission. In fact there had been a series of recon missions conducted at Anzio; one that yielded incomplete intelligence, another that had seen two British commandos captured, and still another on Christmas Eve that had been aborted when the PT boat carrying the recon teams had suffered a malfunction in their radar.

This was a profoundly anxious time for Cus. By this time Evelyn's baby was past due and he had not heard from her. After the briefing, Cus asked and received permission to return to Bizerte, ostensibly to store his excess gear, but also to see if he had any mail. In a 1992 interview with John B. Dwyer and again in a 2002 interview with this author, Cus's commanding officer Ensign L.L. Culver of Tahlequah, Oklahoma recounted the scene when Cus arrived in Bizerte.

"The first thing he did was check his mail," recalled the retired funeral director. "Mail was slow in those days and Cus was anxious to hear from his wife on the birth of their child. He was very happy that a letter from her had arrived. He opened it and read it with a big smile on his face. He grinned from ear to ear. He was a father! It was a girl! Mother and daughter were fine! Pictures were on the way!"

"And then," said Culver "he explained that his wife had written – tongue in cheek I am sure – that she was "sorry" for not giving him a boy and that she would do better next time. He sat on the edge of his bunk with tears in his eyes. He said over and over, 'Oh my poor wife, I can't tell her I'm so happy with a beautiful little girl … but I'll never be able to tell her.'"

"Cus was such a fine young man," Culver concluded. "He was one of those kids that could have done anything he wanted in life - just a fine young man. I've always felt that he had a premonition of his death."

That night Cus and Gene, along with Jim Bligh (who happened to be in port) went out on the town. "Cus was overjoyed," smiled Gene at the memory. "He told anyone within earshot. He had a new baby girl. He was as happy as could be."

"I remember that night well," said Jim Bligh. "The three of us went out for a glass of wine. Cus was so happy, elated as only a new father could be. It was so wonderful to be with him and to hear about his new baby daughter Michelle. It was the last time we ever saw him."

****

The night of December 30, 1943 found Cus at the newly established S&R base on the "Emerald Isle" of Ischia a few miles southwest of the Bay of Naples. The operation was comprised of three two man teams. Capt. W.G. Davis, (RA) and his partner C.S.M. Galloway, Ensign Jerry Donnell and Sub-Lieutenant Williams (RN), and Ensigns Cus Pirro and Ken Howe. Howe, a former physical education instructor in Hannibal Missouri, was an original S&R and had earned a Navy Cross in Operation TORCH. The evening's mission was to gather information on beach gradients, sandbars and water depths at three sectors of beach at Anzio. Capt. Davis was mission OIC. They would operate from PT-201 captained by Lt. George Patterson (USN). At the final briefing they were instructed that if captured they were to say nothing or pretend to be downed airmen.

Each man was issued a waterproof watch, sounding gear, a small compass, pencils and writing tablet, waterproof matches, cigarettes, a .45 caliber pistol and ammunition, a fighting knife and hand grenades. They also stored in their folboats a first-aid kit, water bottles, extra food, spare socks, binoculars, an Italian grammar, some Italian lire, and an escape map. Each man wore sand shoes (canvas rubber soled shoes similar to tennis shoes) and a Mae West life preserver.

By 8:35 pm they were loaded and ready. Patterson's crew cast off and PT-201 slipped quietly from the harbor and set a course for Anzio across the calm Tyrrhenian Sea. With a slight wind and good visibility the sleek torpedo patrol boat made good time. En route the radar went down. But this time Capt. Davis, who had been on the aborted Christmas Eve mission, was confident he could spot land marks without radar and told Patterson to continue. By 11:20pm they arrived off Anzio and Davis sighted and referenced two land marks, the Torre Caldara and the Torre San Lorenzo, silhouetted against the night sky. On the gently rolling deck, the British Captain gathered the teams and quietly gave last minute instructions. The men were to go no closer than 150 yards from shore. They were to take their soundings and return to the PT no later than 3:00 am. At 11:40 pm the deck hands helped the men lower the three folboats over the side. Davis and Galloway first, Pirro and Howe next, Donnell and Williams last. Silently the men dipped their paddles into the water and turned the little boats toward Italy.

Donnell and Williams headed directly shoreward, turned south and paddled 400 yards parallel to the coast. Ashore they could see lights from patrolling sentries. About 150 yards to their north they could barely make out the shape of Pirro and Howe as they arrived at their designated position. Things went smoothly for the pair and by 2:25am they had completed their assignment and were back aboard the PT.

Davis and Galloway had also paddled toward the beach. At 12:20am they sighted a light in the Torre Lorenzo and ten minutes later spied a sentry. By this time the weather was turning foul and they were being pushed seaward. They managed to take their soundings and by 2:40am had joined Donnell and Williams aboard the 201.

With only twenty minutes to go before the prearranged rendezvous time the four men were alarmed that Cus and Howe had not returned. By now a cold rain had started to fall and the men shivered as they stood on the pitching deck and searched in the darkness for their friends. At 2:45 am they saw lights moving along the beach. An hour later, they spotted star shells arching in the rain over the coast. Then in the distance they heard the clatter of gunfire … and then black silence on the "wine dark sea". Michelle's baby pictures were returned unopened.

ANZIO

Gene as an Ensign in Africa, 1943.

XXVII

"God help us.
And don't send Jesus.
This is no place for children."

An Army sergeant's prayer at Anzio.

In the quiet sunrise of January 22, 1943 Major General John P. Lucas stood on the deck of the USS Biscayne and peered through binoculars towards the coast of Anzio three and one-half miles away. He couldn't believe what he was seeing. Ashore his entire VI Corps was quietly wading through gentle surf and landing unopposed on the beaches. Except for a five minute rocket salvo fired by his own forces, there was hardly a shot fired. Filled with relief and confidence the fifty-four year old commander radioed the following to his commanding officer, Gen. Mark Clark, "PARIS-BORDEAUX-TURIN-TANGIERS-BARI-ALBANY," which meant, "Weather clear sea calm, little wind, our presence not discovered. Landings in progress. No reports from landings yet."

By the end of the day the Allies had nearly 40,000 troops, over 3,000 vehicles, and large quantities of matériel landed along a fifteen mile stretch of beach. All three major assault groups were in contact with each other and moving inland. Morale was high, and all hands were confident that the planned rendezvous with their counterparts, who were driving up the Italian peninsula, would be easily achieved.

"The day was sunny and warm," remarked one paratrooper from the 82nd Airborne Division. "It was very hard to believe that a war was going on and I was in the middle of it."

But the young paratrooper had spoken too soon. Despite the fact that he was taken by surprise, Field Marshall Albert Kesselring responded immediately. In a little over six hours he had all or parts of eleven German divisions converging on Anzio to thwart the assault.

Gene's flotilla arrived at the end of the second day. By now Allied supply convoys ferrying men, heavy weapons, ammunition and food, were in high gear and the Luftwaffe, despite attempts to drive them off, had taken to the skies to attack them. In the evening twilight of D+2 over 100 fighter bombers, using radio controlled glide bombs (that had a range of up to ten miles) and radio controlled ballistic bombs (both perfected at Salerno) hit them in a series of continuous raids. One British destroyer was sunk with great loss of life and another disabled. Then, in a act so cruel it is still seared into the memory of all who were there, the Germans targeted three British hospital ships (all of which were clearly illuminated and marked with red crosses), narrowly missing two before scoring a direct hit on and sinking the defenseless HMS St. David.

"I didn't see the St. David go down" said Gene shaking his head. "We heard about it as it happened. But those bastards … those dirty bastards were totally gangsters."

"The air raids were terrible," he went on. "We were shot at and bombed constantly. The problem with an LCT is that they are not maneuverable at all. They weren't nicknamed 'Large Crude Targets' for nothing. You just had to keep going and hope that you didn't get hit. You had no other choice. But I'll tell you, I still don't like to talk about it. Those air raids at Anzio were horrible."

Despite heavy losses, Allied landing craft (with fierce support from naval gunfire) managed to supply a beachhead seven miles deep and fifteen miles long. But by D+4 the situation began to change as a rising wind and mounting seas brought a storm to the area and hindered unloading operations. In the face of the bad weather, the Germans continued to bomb Allied ships and positions and pour troops and armor into the area. As a result, by February 1 the allied attack had stalled. What followed was over four months of protracted savagery that would etch the word Anzio into the annals of battles fought and won at the highest of costs.

For weeks after the initial assault, Gene and his men ferried supplies of all kinds from Liberty ships off shore to the embattled troops in the town and on the beaches. Under constant artillery and aerial bombardment it was grim work.

"We worked twenty-four hours a day," remarked Gene. "Finally I told my commander we needed some relief. We got a few extra guys but I'll tell you, it was tough. We spent weeks at Anzio and were bombed every day. Eventually our troops were able to push inland, but between the air raids, the mines in the water, the submarines and the long hours, Anzio was a tough one … a real tough one."

ENGLAND

Winston Chruchill.

XXVIII

"...we shall never surrender!"

Winston Churchill

Of all the great leaders in world history there were few as charismatic and none more optimistic than Winston Churchill. From the moment his battered army crawled home from Dunkirk - an event he called "a miracle of deliverance", the steadfast prime minister vowed to one day lead them back across the English Channel to victory. His promise was at best, problematic. Indeed, along with the Dunkirk debacle, his forces were kicked out of Europe twice more, at Crete in 1941 and at Dieppe in 1942. But when the Japanese attack at Pearl Harbor brought America into the war the picture changed. By early 1943, plans for a cross channel invasion were underway. The result was an assemblage of men and equipment that defied imagination. By mid 1944 the whole of England had become an armed camp. The coastlines, harbors and beaches were thick with shipping that ranged from battleships, to transports, to dinghies. City streets and country lanes were clogged with tanks, personnel carriers, trucks, jeeps, motorcycles, and artillery pieces. Nearly every acre of large flat ground was converted to airfields packed with bombers, fighters, transports and gliders. And then there were the troops. Millions of them; snaking through the narrow village lanes, maneuvering among the hedgerows and green pastures of the country side, and bobbing around in the cold coastal waters where they practiced coming ashore on the rough and sandy beaches. By the end of May the entire country knew the invasion was on. It was only a matter of when.

Gene arrived in mid April. "We had heard that we were to go home after Anzio," he recalled ruefully. "But on a trip back to Bizerte I broke my ships back. We were coming back to Africa and a storm hit us. I had a light load and headed right into the storm. That was a mistake. LCT's were built in three sections and with no ballast to weight us down the center section actually bent and the thing started to break apart. I had to call for help. They sent a couple of LCI's that hooked up on each side of us and helped us back to Naples. I was lucky to make it to port. Then they towed us all the way across the Med to Bizerte. They had to give me a new ship. They didn't tell me I'd have to go to England to pick it up…the bastards. If I'd have known what was going to happen, I'd have kept the broken one!"

"Before I left," he grinned, "I showed the guy taking over for me, Jim Wilcox, a great guy, where all our booty was stashed. We'd put it all in an empty ballast tank. There were cases of booze, cigarettes, lots of good trade bait. He was a little hesitant but I told him to keep it. What were they going to do, put him in combat?"

"Any way," he continued, "I took four men from my crew and before we knew it we were on an LST bound for England."

It was a great cruise. Across the warm and sunny Mediterranean, through the Straights of Gibraltar to the Atlantic, then up to the United Kingdom to Swansea, Wales before putting into the port town of Penarth near Cardiff. After a year in the swirling violence of a war zone, Wales was like being on another planet. There were dances at the Officers' club, strolls on cobblestone streets, citizens who spoke English, clean restaurants with delicious food, pretty Welsh girls and a pub on every corner.

"We had a great time," smiled Gene. "It had been so long since any of us had seen civilization that we hardly knew how to act."

But despite the luxuries, there were still some shortages, some of them critical.

"I was with three other LCT skippers," explained Gene. "We had come up from Anzio together to pick up our ships. One night we went out for a drink. All of the bartenders were either women or old men since all the young guys were in the service. There was a shortage of hard liquor and the bartenders would only serve it to the locals. We could only get beer. We figured that since we were officers and gentlemen we deserved the hard stuff."

"So anyway," he chuckled, "we went into this Irish pub. I told the other guys to let me do the talking. Inside the place was almost empty except for a few old limeys snuggled up to their drinks. The bartender was an old Irish guy."

With the suave diplomacy of a seasoned LCT'er, Gene went to work.

"Good evening sir," he purred in his terrible Irish brogue. "My friends and I would like a glass of your finest gin."

"Would ye now," trilled the round faced barman.

"Aye, sir, we would."

"Well, I'm sorry to disappoint you lad, but as you know, there's a shortage of fine gin. There's a war on, ye know."

"Shortage you say," answered Gene. "But surely you wouldn't deny an Irish lad and his friends just one glass."

"Oh, Irish is it? Well now, that's different. And where did ye say ye were from lad?"

By this time Gene was in full sales mode, hovering over his own personal island of blarney.

"Why, I'm from County Cork, sir."

"County Cork is it? A fine place that."

"Aye, a fine place indeed – now, about that glass of gin ..."

"Ah yes, the gin. And what'd ye say your name was lad?"

"My name? Why it's O' Benedetti – Geno O'Benedetti."

"When I said that, that old bartender just lit up," Gene grinned years later. "He couldn't help himself. He laughed and laughed. Needless to say, we got our gin."

****

By the time of Gene's arrival, plans for Operation NEPTUNE (the amphibious segment of Operation OVERLORD, the overall invasion of Normandy) were all but complete. Gene was scheduled to take command of an LCT (6). This was good news. Scuttlebutt had it that these newer craft were scheduled to land in the later waves of the assault. But true to form things quickly changed.

"We were in Wales for a very short time," said Gene, "when we got orders to report to something called Gunfire Support Group. I'd never heard of it but when I saw that Captain Sabin was in charge, I knew something was up."

Captain Lorenzo S. Sabin, a native Texan and 1921 graduate of the Naval Academy at Annapolis, was an experienced amphibious man and gunnery expert. In the early stages of the war he served as staff gunnery officer aboard the U.S.S Maryland at Pearl Harbor, and later commanded the Landing Craft Groups in the Mediterranean.

"Captain Sabin was a fine officer," said Gene. "He'd led us in the Med. He was fair and tough … a no bullshit kind of guy. You could talk to him and he'd give you the straight dope. He was a hell of a guy."

Sabin's new command stemmed from a need for greater in-close fire support for assault troops. As a result, a number of aging LCT's were modified for functions beyond that of a landing craft and designated accordingly. LCT (R)'s for rockets ("… something we'd never seen before," remarked Gene.) LCT(G) for ships fitted with two 17 or 25 pound guns, and LCT(A)'s for old mark (5)'s fitted with armor at the bow and wheel house and rigged with wooden platforms to elevate their tanks so they could fire over the side while underway. As the multifunctional group came together, Sabin discovered a need for experienced skippers.

"He had a bunch of ninety-day wonders with no real experience," explained Gene. "He went down the list of skippers in England and saw our names. Since we'd served under him in the Med, he knew what we could do. He had enough influence to transfer us to his group. He gave me command of LCT(A) #2228. We took it over just in time for one of the dry runs at Slapton Sands."

During the pre-invasion buildup Allied planners scheduled two full scale rehearsals for NEPTUNE, one in late April and the other in early May. Conducted along a stretch of beach in southern England called Slapton Sands, they were designed to simulate as closely as possible actual combat conditions. During the April exercise, known as Operation TIGER, a flotilla of eight LST's transporting follow-up troops and equipment was making its way toward the rehearsal beach when a squadron of nine German Schnellboote (torpedo boats) appeared out of the darkness and attacked. One LST was heavily damaged, another burst into flames and still another was sunk outright. The total loss of life was 749. It was the most costly training exercise in WWII.

"That incident really woke people up," said Gene. "It let a lot of the green troops know that it was going to be a tough go."

For Gene the transfer to Sabin's command was a mixed blessing.

"I knew and trusted Captain Sabin," said Gene. "He was a good man to serve under. But after all that had happened in the Med, I had no real desire to be in the initial waves. Sabin called us into his cabin for a private briefing. He knew we were not up to speed as to what was happening since we'd only been in England for a short time. He told us about the beaches, and also about the armament."

'You'll be heading into a dead beach Gene,' he said. 'The rockets from the LCT (R)'s will fire over your heads. Don't be afraid. They'll make a lot of noise, but they'll go over your heads and blast the hell out of the beach. Between the air force, the rockets and the naval bombardment, the beach will be dead. There won't be a shot fired at you.'

"I believed him," said Gene. "He believed what he was saying, too. When he told us we were assigned to a beach called Omaha, I didn't think anything of it. He had no way of knowing what was going to happen."

Thus assured, Gene found himself anchored on the River Dart at the old port of Dartmouth in command of LCT (A) 210.

"My first ship developed some engine trouble so at the last minute they gave me another one," explained Gene. "It was an old LCT that we'd lend leased to the British. They'd loaned it back to us for the invasion. It had been fitted with armor at the bow and around the wheel house. They'd built wooden platforms about four feet high on the deck to hold three Sherman tanks. At the bow, there were two 300 lb. extension ramps that had to be flipped down so the tanks could drive off when we hit shore. It was quite a deal. Anyway, I took my guys aboard and we anchored at the mouth of the Dart River. Every day the tide would go out and we'd be high and dry in the mud. There wasn't much to do. All we could do now was wait."

****

Across the channel in France, the Germans were also waiting. Since early 1943, Hitler knew that a cross channel invasion was inevitable. His response was to build a string of fortifications along the coast of Western Europe called the "Atlantic Wall." In November, he put Field Marshall Erwin Rommel in charge of inspecting and fortifying the wall along the Kanalkuste (Channel coast).

The son of a school teacher, Rommel had served the Fatherland since his days as a cadet at the Royal Officer School in Danzig in 1910. During the First World War he fought with distinction on the western front where he earned an Iron Cross (first and second class) and the coveted Pour le Mérite. A career officer, teacher and military author he was a disciplined and professional warrior. He was not a Nazi. At the outbreak of the war his star rose when he led the 7th Panzer Division to sweeping victories in France. His exploits brought a promotion to General and command of the vaunted Afrika Corps that drove England's 8th Army out of Libya. Although defeated at El Alamein and driven from Tunisia by the Allies, the legendary "Desert Fox" remained a charismatic and respected leader. He was Germany's finest solider.

Rommel, "The Desert Fox."

Like nearly all the German high command, Rommel assumed that the invasion would come at Pas-de-Calais. It faced the narrowest part of the channel and, if taken, offered a straight route to Berlin. Moreover, Hitler had built launching sites for his V-1 and V-2 weapons in the area and the allies considered them a priority target. Consequently, the highest concentrations of defenses were constructed in Calais, and the best available troops were assigned to defend it. (In fact German leaders were duped by Allied counter-intelligence into believing that the actual invasion was a diversion and thus kept their troops at Calais for weeks after D-Day waiting for the "real" invasion).

But Rommel also realized that the Allies might invade elsewhere and saw the coast of Normandy as a potential landing site. He took particular interest in a six-mile stretch of crescent shaped beach between the villages of Vierville on the west and

Colleville on the east. Bordered by cliffs on each end and overlooked by thirty-foot high bluffs, the golden strand was narrow and enclosed. Rommel saw at once that it could not be out-flanked and was a perfect place to defend. He also recognized that if the Allies did land in Normandy they would have to include this beach. If they came ashore here, he concluded, he could defeat them at the waters edge and push them back into the sea. Employing all the defensive lessons he had learned in World War One, he put his men to work.

In expectation of an attack at high tide, hundreds of mine-tipped tetrahedrons (called "Hedgehogs" by the Allies) anchored in concrete and designed to explode on contact were placed offshore so they could not be detected by incoming craft. Large obstructions called "Belgian Gates" designed to rip the bottom out of landing craft were sunk just beneath the water's surface. On the beach, thousands of mines and anti-tank obstacles were buried in the sand. On the bluffs, twelve reinforced concrete bunkers holding pre-sighted 88mm and 75mm guns looked down on every foot of the strand. Between the bunkers, miles of concertina wire were strung and trenches were dug and filled with troops armed with everything from rifles to high-caliber machine guns. Behind the beaches, artillery batteries stood ready to blast incoming troops at the waterline.

The Desert Fox knew how to garrison and defend a position. When he was done, every square yard of the beach the Allies called Omaha was enfiladed into an impregnable and murderous killing ground.

D-DAY JUNE 6, 1944

A seasoned skipper.

XXIV

"Oh hear us as we cry to Thee,
For those in peril on the sea!"

From The Navy Hymn
By Rev. William Whiting

Operation OVERLORD got off to a sporadic start. "We went out the night before," recalled Gene, "but the weather was so bad that we were called back. It was a real mess, all of those ships returning and having to refuel. But the next night Eisenhower said it was a go and the invasion was on."

"It was a massive, massive thing," he said about the largest armada ever assembled. "It is impossible for me to describe how big it was. We got out into the channel to the rendezvous site, (a pre-arranged point off the coast called "Piccadilly Circus") and formed up. I had three Sherman tanks and their crews and about 140 combat engineers aboard. We headed out for France. All around us were thousands of ships. And overhead we could hear our planes. It was an enormous undertaking - just enormous!"

The 5-knot per hour trip through the rough seas took its toll on the men.

"Going over the men on deck really suffered," said Gene. "Most of them had not been aboard a small craft and they got very sea sick. With the extra weight of the armor, that old LCT had very little freeboard and we shipped a lot of water. The men were wet, cold, miserable and puking. They were all pretty quiet and also pretty scared."

"I'd gone into Dartmouth the day before we left," he went on, "looking for some gin to take along. The town was so crowded you could hardly walk on the street. There wasn't a drop of gin in the entire town! I had to settle for scotch. I hate scotch. But I bought it anyway."

"During the crossing I'd duck below every so often to take a drink. At the last minute in Dartmouth some officer had came aboard as an observer. Why or for what reason I do not know, since all he did was stay below. When I came down for a drink he kind of looked at me funny. Hell, I didn't care. It helped to calm my nerves. And anyway, what the hell was he going to do about it?"

The invasion beaches at Normandy ran along a forty mile stretch of coastline from the base of the Cotentin peninsula at Quineville in the west to Cabourg at the mouth of the Dives River in the east. Approaching from the sea, the American beaches from right to left and were code named Utah and Omaha, respectively. Further to the left the British and Canadian sectors were designated Gold, Juno and Sword.

Omaha beach was about six miles long and separated into four main sectors. Approaching from the sea they were from right to left; Charlie, Dog, Easy and Fox. Each sector was further separated and designated from right to left; Dog Green, Dog White, Dog Red, Easy Green, Easy Red, Fox Green and Fox Red.

For months prior to D-day allied bombers had devastated the Nazis. In February alone over 6,000 sorties had dropped over 18,000 tons of bombs on Germany. A full one-third of Herman Goering's Luftwaffe was lost. With air superiority established, Allied forces approached Omaha with optimism.

LCT 210. Taken in the Med in 1943, the 210 carried Gene and his crew into Omaha.

The plan called for an air force bombardment, followed by a naval shelling, after which LCT (R)'s would rain thousands of rockets on any hapless survivors. The coup de' grace would be delivered by 40,000 men and 3,000 vehicles that would storm ashore, scale the bluffs, and take out any remaining resistance. Intelligence reports indicated the beach was defended by a second-rate battalion of conscripted Poles and Russians. No one expected any problems.

When the curtain went up the plan went awry. Flying in bad weather, the B-17's arrived late, over flew the beach and dropped their bombs three miles inland. Concentrating their fire on the nearly indestructible bunkers, the Navy's cannonade did minimal damage. The rockets fired from the LCT (R)'s, although loud and spectacular, fell short, and exploded harmlessly in the surf.

Moreover, Omaha was defended by three battalions of first rate troops. Thus as the sun rose on D-day, the most impregnable landing area in the entire sector stood professionally defended and virtually untouched.

As the gray dawn began to illuminate the coastline Gene looked shoreward.

"We knew about the beach obstacles," he said. "We came in at low tide to avoid them. My landmark was a church steeple between Coleville and Vierville." (Accounts vary as to the 210's actual location. Gene's recollection would have put him somewhere in the Dog Red sector). "The seas were pretty rough and about a mile out our rudder cable broke. I dropped our stern anchor. I knew if we got in trouble and with the rudder malfunctioning I could use the anchor to get off the beach. I could see the steeple in the distance. I had expected it to be destroyed but it was not touched. And it didn't look like anything else had hit the beach either."

The church between Colleville and Viervielle as it appears today. "I could see the steeple in the distance."
Courtesy Claus Jessen.

As the 210 drew closer to shore a precursor to what lay ahead floated by on the rising tide.

"As we approached we saw troops floating in their life jackets in the water," said Gene. "Those poor bastards. They were tankers from the DD tanks. They were tanks that had been fitted with rubber skirts so they floated. They had duel drives and were supposed to operate like a boat. They were supposed to land before us but the guys in them couldn't handle the rough seas. Some of them got ashore and did good work. But many of them swamped and a lot of their guys were lost. We were instructed to not pick up survivors. They were picked up later by rescue boats."

Omaha beach where Gene landed as it appears today.
Courtesy Claus Jessen.

By now the tension aboard was palatable. The four men on the anti-aircraft guns, their weapons locked and loaded, searched the gray skies for enemy planes. The two men at the helm (one to steer and the other to handle the throttles) fought to stay on course as the current drove them to the left of their landfall. Aft, two more sailors manned the stern anchor as the long cable played out behind them. Forward, a single bowman prepared to engage the winch that lowered the main ramp. On each side of the bow, two more blue jackets got ready to throw over the steel plate extensions for the tanks. Up on the platforms the tankers of the 743rd Battalion revved their engines as their gunners peered ashore looking for targets.

Meanwhile, down on the main deck, officers and NCO's barked last minute instructions as the young combat engineers stood in the wet spray, swallowed their sea sickness, and whispered quiet prayers. Their job was to wade through the shallow water at low tide, blow up the beach obstacles and mark a fifty-yard wide pathway for boats coming in on later waves.

Overhead, thousands of rockets fired from Sabin's LCT (R)'s shrieked past on their way to shore. Behind them, scores of LCI's churned shoreward. The boys in them (part of the 116th Regimental Combat Team) hailed from Virginia and Maryland and were descendents of the fabled Stonewall Brigade from the American Civil War.

Five minutes before touchdown the salvo stopped.

"Everything was quiet," recalled Gene. "All you could hear were the engines and the water slapping the sides of the ship. Not a round was fired at us."

Then the ramp went down.

"It was like the entire world exploded in our faces," said Gene softly. "We never had a chance."

The 210 was one of the very first LCT's to beach. Every German gun in the sector zeroed in and opened up with murderous accuracy. From the trenches on the bluff, small arms and machine gun fire ripped into the bodies of the men as they stumbled down the ramp and fell dead and wounded in the chill water. From the bunkers, 75mm and dreaded 88's rained down on the hapless men, the shock of their explosions piercing the air, their shrapnel tearing through the crowded craft. A minute later spotters on the bluff radioed co-ordinates to artillery batteries a few miles behind the beach. Within seconds more 88's were bracketing the 210 with withering fire.

From the bridge Gene watched in horror as his helpless ship rocked and trembled from direct hits fore and aft.

"They shot out two engines almost at once," he said. "Up front they hit us on both sides of the bow. Two of the kids who were supposed to throw over the ramp extensions were killed, and two more were wounded."

Things quickly got worse.

"When the two kids were killed, fires broke out on each side of the bow," he said quietly. "The soldiers were struggling through the fires trying to get off. They were getting shot in the water. The ramp extensions were still up and the tanks couldn't get off the ship."

Without hesitation, Gene raced down from the bridge. The two wounded men were helped to the rear. The dead were dragged away. And then alone under intense fire, Gene single handedly muscled the 300lb. ramp extensions into place.

"In situations like that you'll do whatever you have to," he said sixty years later. We had to get those tanks off. We had to get off the beach. They were going to kill us all. There was no other choice."

With the ramp extensions in place the three tanks lumbered through the smoke and flames into the surf. By this time other LCT's were beaching.

"Looking back that may have helped us," said Gene. "We were burning and the krauts started to zero in on other targets. We had dragged the dead and wounded away from the bow. It seemed like it took hours to put the fires out (it was probably about 45 minutes). I couldn't pull off the beach until they were extinguished. Finally we got them out. I ordered us off the beach. Thank God my stern anchor was out. We managed to slowly retract. God, what a mess!"

By the time the 210 retreated to the relative safety of the channel, the attack was in full swing. Now operationally ineffective, Gene radioed his plight to his superiors.

"I called Captain Sabin's control boat and reported our situation," he said. "He ordered us to one of the floating dry docks offshore. He said he'd send a smaller boat to pick us up with our wounded. He also ordered me to bury my dead. At that moment there was no time and no place to process the dead. That was one of the toughest things I've ever had to do."

In a scene of heartbreaking sadness the battered little ship hove too in the pitching seas and the bloodied crew gathered around the bodies of their fallen comrades.

Gene's eyes filled with tears as he recounted the moment.

"I said the Lords prayer," he whispered. "I asked God to bless and keep their souls. I said a prayer for their families. And then we dropped them over the side."

The day wasn't over.

"When we got back to the big ship," said Gene, "Captain Sabin asked us if anyone felt like going go back in. He said no one had to go… but the men on the beach needed ammunition. We knew those guys were taking a real beating. So I and a couple of others said we'd go back in a smaller boat with ammo."

The only time Gene recalls wearing his Silver Star was when it was pinned on him at Camp Bradford, VA.

The return trip was a ghastly and bloody postscript to the morning's terror.

"Oh God, it was awful," said Gene softly. "By that time the tide had risen and we could go right up to shore. I had to put a man up front with a staff to push the bodies out of the way. The water was actually red with blood. When we got to the beach we were still fired upon. The three tanks we had landed were all blown up. All of the men we'd landed were dead. I just don't like to talk about it."

For his actions that morning Gene Benedetti was awarded the Silver Star for Valor Under Fire.

"To this day," he said years later, "I do not know why they gave me that medal. I don't think I ever wore it. I was no hero. The heroes were the kids we left on the beach."

"That day," he concluded, "was the worst and longest day of my life. After Normandy, I never think about yesterday – and I never worry about tomorrow."

BUCKSKIN BENEDETTI
October 1944

Gene and Evelyn, circa 1945.

XXX

"There was only one guy in the world whose neck came right out of his shoulders."

Jim Bligh

The bus was slow. And the two lane road made it even slower. But there was nothing one could do, so Jim Bligh waited impatiently behind the wheel of his car and watched as it slowly disgorged its passengers in front of the main gate at Camp Bradford on a bright autumn day in Virginia.

Since graduating from the Tunney Program in the summer of 1942, Bligh's naval career had been busy. After his marriage to Betty O'Brien the following February he'd shipped out to the Mediterranean and served on Admiral Hewitt's staff for the Sicily and the Salerno invasions. By mid 1944 he'd rotated back to the states, completed midshipmen's school at Columbia University and was now serving on a mine sweeper at the Navy's sprawling facility at Little Creek.

"After my transfer to mine sweepers Betty came down and we rented a place in Norfolk," he said. "That's where I was headed when I stopped behind the bus. I was just sitting there when I saw the back of this guy whose head came straight out of his shoulders. I couldn't believe it. There was only one guy in the whole world that looked like that. I knew immediately who it was. I got out of my car and yelled, 'That looks like Buckskin Benedetti!'"

"Gene could never remember people's names," he explained. "He always called everyone 'Buckskin' or 'Buck.' When I called out to him he stopped and without even turning around yelled back in that deep voice of his, 'That sounds like Bligh!'.

"Evelyn was beautiful. And Michelle was the most amazing child I'd ever seen."

It was a moment of unrestrained joy.

"Oh it was so good to see him," Jim went on. "I had not heard from him and I knew he'd been at Normandy. I knew the LCT's had been in the thick of it. I was so glad to see him alive! We must have stopped traffic for five minutes just hugging each other."

Gene's return to the states had also been a circuitous one.

"After the morning of D-day," he said, "we'd secured the beaches by the end of the day. I got a new ship and stayed on station for a few weeks ferrying supplies to the beach. About two weeks after the assault we got hit by a terrible storm that knocked out our temporary harbor and did a lot of other damage. Finally my back gave out. I'd torn it up handling those damn ramp extensions. I landed in the hospital in England. I was waiting to be operated on when I got my orders to go home. I told the doctor to keep his operation. I wanted to come home. I came back on one of the United States liners. It was a great trip, I can tell you."

"When I got back," he went on, "my initial orders were to go out to the Pacific. I wasn't real happy with that. I felt I'd done enough. So the commanding officer asked me if I knew anything about barrage balloons. When I told him I'd seen them at Normandy, he said that qualified me as an expert and put me in charge of a barrage balloon class. Eventually he made me a training officer. Camp Bradford was the big LCT training base and that's where I was going when I heard Jim's voice. What a great surprise!"

Evelyn was always beautiful...

"It was so good to see Gene," remembered Jim. "I took him to our little house in Norfolk to see Betty. We had a spare bedroom and he stayed with us."

"We explained to him that Betty's best friend Evelyn was coming to visit," Jim continued. "She was Cus Pirro's wife. We were pretty sure that Cus was not coming back. Betty had invited Eve down so we could be with her when the word came. Anyway, we asked Gene if he would come to dinner with us so that she wouldn't be alone - so that she wouldn't feel like a third wheel."

... and always stylish. So was Gene.

"I said sure," said Gene. "I couldn't tell her what happened to Cus because none of us knew. But I could tell her that I'd seen him and that when I did he was fine."

Cus's disappearance had been devastating for Evelyn and the entire Pirro family.

"When it happened," remembered Evelyn, "I was inconsolable. I could not accept Cus being gone. It was just unspeakable. I had trouble controlling my emotions. So when Jim suggested I come down to visit I stalled. But he thought it would be good for me to not be alone. So I got my mother to baby-sit and went to Little Creek anyway. Afterwards I was glad I did. It was good for me."

"We all went out to dinner at the Officer's Club," recalled Gene. "I'll never forget it. She was so beautiful. I was amazed. We just talked and chatted. I told her what I knew about Cus, how often I'd seen him, that we'd played basketball and softball and volleyball together in between invasions. At this time he was still reported as missing. I knew what she was going through because my brother Dan was still missing. I knew how tough it was for her. I just told her to try and remain positive. That was pretty much the end of it."

"He was really a nice guy," said Evelyn of that first evening. "He talked about his family so much. He was polite and nice and very consoling. I liked him for that. He understood. But there was nothing romantic; he was just a nice guy and we had a good conversation and I appreciated his company."

****

On May 7, 1945 Germany surrendered and the war in Europe was mercifully over. Out in the Pacific, the Japanese remained defiant. But by the end of June, after vicious fighting and numbing casualties of both sides, Iwo Jima and Okinawa had fallen. The defeat of Japan was only a matter of time.

Gene spent these months as a training officer on the east coast.

"I was based at Camp Bradford," he said. "My job was to travel up and down the coast and set up and keep track of training programs for new LCT skippers. We were getting ready to invade Japan and they figured they would need a lot of new skippers. It was a good job. I even got to train some Russians. I went all over, up to New York, down to Florida ... all up and down the coast."

He also continued to see Evelyn.

"After V-E Day (May 8, 1945) Cus was declared dead," said Evelyn. "I was very sad of course, but also somewhat relieved to have it over. I had known in my heart that he was gone. Now I knew for sure. I was still pretty shaky. But in a way it was a sense of relief to have it over."

"Right around that time," said Gene, "she came down for a visit and we went to dinner again with Jim and Betty. Evie felt a little better that she had an answer about Cus. On the way back from dinner she said, 'well, when you come up to Washington, come in and meet my family.'"

Family Day at the base.

"I had some ships at Solomon Island in Maryland," he explained. "That was only about twenty-five miles from Silver Springs where Evie was living with her parents."

"So anyway," he went on, "the next time I was up there I called her and she asked me to come over and meet her Mom and Dad."

It was a clash of cultures and Gene laughed at the memory of his first trip to the Birrel home.

"At the time everything was still rationed," he explained. "So I took along a bunch of food, meat and butter, stuff that was difficult to get. Evie's mom was real happy to get all the food, but down at the bottom of the bag I had a quart of Christian Brother's brandy. I didn't know that her mom was a strict Southern Methodist and didn't allow liquor in the house. It was a little awkward. But Evie's Dad, Tope, he thought it was great. He took it for himself."

"It wasn't the smoothest start," he concluded, "but it went all right. Besides, I was there to see Evie and Michelle. Michelle was the most beautiful little girl I'd ever seen. She was amazing - just a beautiful child."

In fact, Gene was in love.

"Deep in my heart I knew Evie was the one for me," he said. "But I didn't know what to do. She was so beautiful. She was so nice and charming. Michelle was such a beautiful little girl. I wasn't sure how to handle it all. And I didn't know how she felt about me. But boy, in my heart I was really taken. I knew I loved her. There was no question about it."

Evelyn was understandably cautious.

"After all that had happened - after Cus - I was not sure," she said. "I was still very young and so much had happened. I knew I liked Ben (his Navy buddies called him "Bennie" she explained. I didn't like that so I called him Ben). I enjoyed his company. But beyond that I wasn't sure."

****

As the end of the war drew near leaders were faced with the task of how to smoothly discharge and assimilate nearly 12 million service personnel (over 7 million of them stationed overseas) back into society. Too rapid a demobilization, they feared, would flood the job market with returning veterans, lead to massive layoffs, and weaken the economy with runaway inflation. To ensure an orderly transition to peacetime, a point system was devised. All service personnel were awarded points based on length of duty, number of months spent overseas, combat records (medals and battle stars) and family status (married and number of children under the age of 18). Points were tabulated on each man's "adjusted service rating card". When a man accumulated eighty-five points he was sent home.

"When the point system was initiated I knew I wasn't getting out for while, recalled Gene. "Even with making all the invasions and being in combat the key thing was marriage and kids. I was single. I figured to be in for at least another year, maybe more."

"I was so ready to get out," he went on. "I had been corresponding with Dick Blewett, my old football coach at the junior college. He told me that he had a job coaching and teaching if I could get back by the first of September. Coaching had been my dream but I had to tell him that I didn't have the points."

But like everything in his Navy experience, things changed rapidly.

"I was sitting on board one of my ships one day when the kid working the radio took a message about a new ALLNAV (a Navy regulation) that had just become effective. He brought it up to me and said, 'Skipper, I think this might interest you.' I couldn't believe what I was reading. It said that anyone with a Congressional Medal of Honor, the Navy Cross or the Silver Star was eligible for immediate discharge, no questions asked!"

"I was ecstatic," he went on. "I went up to the communications officer and had him verify it. Then I went to my boss, Captain Matthews, and told him I was going home."

'Like hell you are,' he told Gene.

"Like hell I'm not," Gene answered. "Verify the ALLNAV, I'm going home."

"Captain Matthews was a bang bang kind of guy," explained Gene. "He picked up the phone right there and checked it out. He was really teed-off. He told me I'd be traveling without orders but I told him not to worry about it, I was going home."

"Anyway, he had to give in. In truth he was a great guy. He got me an advance on my pay and I started packing my stuff."

But there was still some unfinished business.

"I called Evelyn and told her I was being discharged," Gene said. "I told her I was coming up to Washington to catch the Navy plane home. So I went to her house and stayed for a couple of days with her family."

There wasn't much time.

"We talked at length," he went on. "I asked her if she was serious."

"It all moved pretty fast," Evelyn recalled of those two days. "I told him that I cared for him deeply. That I enjoyed his company but that I was not serious enough to commit to anything. I felt that I cared for him but I wasn't sure if I loved him. So much had happened. He didn't press. We agreed that he would go home and that we'd stay in touch and just see where it led."

"I was comfortable with that," said Gene. "I knew we should not move too fast. But I also knew I loved her."

There was also another matter to settle before leaving. Although he was reported missing in action in 1942, Gene's older brother Dante had never been found. It is impossible to overstate the family's bereavement, especially for Gene's mother, Pia.

"Dan's disappearance was tearing my mother apart," said Gene. "It was very tough on her. She just could not accept that he was gone. She expected him to walk through the door every day. I knew he was gone. I'd know in my heart from the very beginning. But my mother ... well, she never gave up."

"So anyway," he went on, "before I left, Evie and I went to the War Department in Washington. I spoke to the Marine liaison in the bureau of personnel. I told him to write a letter to my mother telling her that Dan was dead. I had to. I knew it would break her heart, but the uncertainty was just killing her. I told him to date the letter to arrive after I got home. I wanted to be with her when she got the news. The next day I caught the plane home. My war was finally over."

****

For the Benedetti and Pirro families the end of the war was bittersweet. While each knew the joy of a son coming home, each also suffered the devastating sorrow of a son forever lost. While Dante John Benedetti and Carmon Francis Pirro never returned in body, their spirits linger still. For like all heroes they, and the brave who fell with them, left an everlasting repousse of honor and courage, in the hearts of their families, in the memories of those who knew them, and in the history of the grateful nation they so nobly served.

"It was guys like Dan and Cus who were the heroes of the war," said Gene. "They are the ones who taught us all the price of freedom."

December 1945
Cotati, California

Gene looked dapper and Evie was stunning.

XXXI

"He made it sound like the Ponderosa."

Evelyn Benedetti

Gene and Evelyn were married in a quiet Catholic ceremony on Saturday December 22, 1945 at tiny St. Joseph's Church in Cotati, California. Gene wore a dark double-breasted business suit with white shirt and French-cuffs. Evelyn was beautiful in an elegant suit, stylish hat and stunning Canadian mink coat. Gene's sister Milli served as Evelyn's matron of honor and his brother-in-law, Red stood as best man. After the ceremony the guests, including Evelyn's father Gordon who had come all the way from Washington DC, gathered in the basement of the family home for a small reception. The intimate day was the start of a marriage that would last forever.

Gene's pursuit of Evelyn had begun the moment he had arrived home the previous summer.

"When I got back the first thing I did was go to the Junior College to nail down a job," he said. "My old coach Dick Blewett had promised me a coaching and teaching position and he came through. I started working immediately. I knew I needed an income to support Evie. Now all I had to do was get her out to California.

So I wrote her a love letter every day. After a while, she couldn't resist."

Evelyn tells it differently.

"A letter," she scoffed. "It was more like a telegram. I'd get a two-liner from Western Union ... 'Darling, we play so-and-so. Pray for us. Love Ben. The next day it was ... 'Darling, we won. Hooray, Love Ben.' But a letter ... hardly."

"She just doesn't remember," Gene laughingly protested. "I wrote her and told her all about the ranch and California and everything. I gave her a very honest and accurate description of the ranch. Hey, I loved her. I had to tell her how it was."

Evelyn laughed out loud at the memory.

"Oh please. He's full of it," she mocked. "His letters, (when he actually wrote one) and his descriptions on the phone made the place sound like the Ponderosa. 'Come to California, come to the "spread." We've got cattle, we've got horses. Come out to the beautiful ranch. We're just outside San Francisco. I just bought a brand new car. I love you. I'll dress you in diamonds.'"

"To hear him tell it" she went on, "he wrote like Lord Byron and lived like landed gentry. Boy was I fooled."

But in truth, she couldn't resist.

"I knew I loved Ben," she said seriously, "but I was naturally apprehensive. So much had happened in both of our lives and I knew it was risky. But I sensed that we could make it work. Even so, it was a huge decision. After all, I was a widow and a single mother. In those days a woman in my position just didn't pack up and move across the county."

"But," she shrugged, "I was very young and felt that I didn't have much of a life back east. So I decided to go to California and start a new life. After all that had happened, I felt that the least I could do was try. I went up to visit Cus' parents in New York and told them my decision. They were very understanding, although I knew they would miss Michelle. But the war had changed all of our lives. We all wanted to look ahead – look to the future. I left on November 2nd and flew to Los Angeles."

To say the least, Evelyn's arrival was an awakening.

"I couldn't believe Los Angeles," she laughed. "What a change! It was cold and wintry when we left D.C. I was dressed in woolen clothes with a fur coat and had dressed Michelle in a matching outfit - that's how one dressed little girls in those days, matching outfits - and we got to LA and it was warm, like summer! So I started peeling off poor little Michelle's winter clothes. Then we got on the plane for San Francisco and they announced that it was cold and raining up there, so I had to bundle her up again. When we finally arrived, Ben met us at the airport.

Cutting the cake.

"She's right," said Gene proudly. "I picked them up in my new car."

Evelyn quickly discovered that to Gene, "new" was a relative term.

"He had written me that he had a brand new car," she laughed. "And he did. The only problem was that it had been new to a lot of people before him. It was a bucket of bolts! It was a wonder he managed to get it to the airport!"

Along with the car, Gene's sense of geography was also open to interpretation.

Evelyn's father Gordon "Topah" came all the way from D.C.

"He had repeatedly told me that his ranch was 'just outside San Francisco'," said Evelyn. "So we're driving through The City in a driving rain – I mean you could hardly see in the dark – when we got to the end of Van Ness Avenue I thought we were coming to the ranch. But then he turned onto the Golden Gate Bridge and I thought, 'where is he taking me?'"

After a wet, vision-impaired trip up the Old Redwood Highway, Gene's "new car" wheezed and rattled into Cotati and slewed down the muddy road to the main house of the Benedetti "spread." It was another awakening and Evelyn still smiles at the memory.

"Let's just say it was one of those incidents where you imagine what something looks like but the reality is completely different," she laughed ruefully. "But we were there, and I met Ben's parents and family for the first time."

After the wedding the couple moved into the small guest cabin (it's still there) adjacent to Giacondo and Pia's house. For a city girl like Evelyn, it was a time of manifold adjustment.

"I had never lived on a ranch before," she recalled. "All of it was new to me. What a different life!"

The morning gathering; "It was all so new to me."

"It was new for her," agreed Gene. "But she jumped right in and helped. We gathered eggs together; I showed her how I milked the cows and all the stuff we did on the ranch. It was fun."

But it wasn't Xanadu. In fact, in the clannish culture of a traditional Italian home, Evelyn was viewed askance, especially by Pia and Milli.

"It would be less than honest to say that I was warmly accepted at first," said Evelyn. "Ben's mother was still very upset over losing Dante. Plus, I wasn't Italian, I'd been married before and I had a child. These were all factors to her. She and Milli spoke Italian in the kitchen and I didn't. I'd try to help but couldn't really communicate. I was a definite outsider and felt like one. It took a while, and eventually we became very close. But it was very difficult at first."

Gene confirmed: "At first my mother had opposed my marrying Evie. She was worried that I wouldn't get along with Michelle. I told her to not worry about that. Michelle was the most wonderful little girl I'd ever seen. She was also apprehensive because Evie was from a different background. The fact that Evie had been married before and had a baby mattered to her. I told her not to worry about that either. Those things didn't matter to me, but my mother was old-fashioned that way. My dad was indifferent, he didn't care. So it was very tough on Evie at first. But after a while it all worked out."

"She pitched in and helped."

Domestic adjustments notwithstanding, the couple settled into married life. For Gene things had never looked better and the future was bright. He was home, had married the woman he loved, and was doing the work he had trained for all of his life.

"I loved coaching and teaching," he recalled. "I had spent all of my spare time overseas compiling playbooks for football. When I got back, I had two or three big notebooks full of plays. It was all I wanted to do. We had a great team at the JC in 1945. (The Bear Cubs went undefeated with one tie and won a championship). I was never happier. I had Evie and Michelle and the job of my dreams."

And so with the confidence that comes with having ones' life in perfect order, Gene accepted an invitation to speak at a sports banquet in Petaluma in February of 1946. As he took his seat at the head table in the American Legion Hall the older man sitting next to him offered his hand and introduced himself. His name was George A. Dondero. He was the General Manager of the Petaluma Cooperative Creamery, and he was about to change Gene's life.

A walk in The City.

THE CO-OP

The original Petaluma Co-operative Creamery

XXXII

"A creamery of the dairyman;
by the dairyman;
for the dairyman . . ."

Petaluma Cooperative Creamery slogan, 1936

As the story goes, one day in early 1913 a local dairyman named Silvio Gambonini and a creamery manager from San Luis Obispo named W.B. Hopkins rode out to the corner of 'D' and Lakeville streets in Petaluma to scout for a suitable building site. As the two men sat together a passing train rumbled by, blew its whistle and spooked their horses. Chagrined, they decided that the vacant lot by the tracks would not do and decided to look elsewhere. They settled on the empty corner of Western and Baker streets. Before long, a new building began to take shape. When it was finished a local sign painters' work told passers-by that the barn shaped structure with the large loading dock was the Petaluma Co-operative Creamery. Soon thereafter, the clip-clop of horse-drawn wagons and the rattling clank of ten-gallon milk cans became a familiar sound in the quiet streets as they made their way to the town's newest business.

The creamery's origins could be traced to two events that occurred in the mid-1800's. One was the discovery of gold, which brought an influx of prospectors who, along with their lust for wealth, sought the protein and nutrients found in dairy products. The other was the subsequent growth of San Francisco, which had exploded almost overnight from a quiet pueblo on the Golden Gate Straight, into a raucous and rumbling city flexing Americas' muscles of freedom and opportunity. For the Irish, Italian and Swiss dairymen forty miles up the coast on Tomales Bay the new market was a godsend. When a ship came to call, they hoisted flags on the hillsides to signal their fellow dairymen that it was time to haul their heavy crates of butter down to the docks to be taken south to market.

But over time the bay at Tomales began to fill with silt causing local commerce to move inland where Chinese laborers, with the help of puffing steam excavators (and later the Army Corps of Engineers) had straightened and deepened the Petaluma Creek. By 1880, steamships like Alma and Steamer Gold were regularly chugging up and down the once meandering tidewater slough and transporting goods and passengers to points south.

By the dawn of the 20th century, dairy farming was changing dramatically. Improved irrigation, the introduction of alfalfa, which was considered a miracle feed, more efficient herd management and better breeding practices allowed farmers to produce a finer product. Technological innovations like the cream separator, the milking machine and nascent refrigeration techniques had transformed the business from a primitive one, into one that was scientific and modern. Even so, running a dairy farm remained a demanding business. Cows had to be milked every twelve hours, leaving little time for much else. Furthermore, milk is perishable, heavy and difficult to transport, especially by horse drawn wagon on the rough country lanes of the day. And even if he found the time to separate his milk into cream and churn it to butter, a farmer had no viable way to mass market his product. Finally, quality varied from herd to herd making it difficult to produce a consistent product and establish a stable price.

Gambonini and Hopkins recognized these variables and saw the burgeoning San Francisco market as an infinite opportunity. Toward that end, the two men decided to combine their resources. Hopkins, who had many business contacts, traveled to San Francisco looking for a buyer, while Gambonini made the rounds in his native north coast hunting for investors. When the two were done, Hopkins had procured the services of a wholesale butter distributor and Gambonini had convinced thirty-two of his fellow dairymen to put up enough money to form a cooperative. Thus on September 12, 1913, California Secretary of State Frank C. Jordan, certified the groups articles of corporation and put the new enterprise officially in business.

It was an immediate success. With six employees churning cream from 1,900 cows, the new creamery shipped 200,000 pounds of butter in its first year of operation. In 1917, George Dondero arrived on the scene. A native San Franciscan, Dondero's management skills were "loaned" to the creamery from a commission house in The City. The "loan" turned into a permanent position and over time the dynamic young manager rose through the ranks to assume the position of General Manager. A talented and visionary leader, Dondero had helped guide the business through the tumultuous events of the First World War, the crippling financial era of the Great Depression and the drastic manpower shortages of World War Two. By the time he introduced himself to Gene Benedetti, he headed-up one of the largest and most successful businesses in the region, producing and shipping a wide variety of dairy products throughout much of northern California.

"I'd heard of him," said Gene of that first encounter. "But I had no idea why he was there, other than the fact that he was very involved in the community and was a sports fan."

With his past reputation as an athlete, and his service in the war, Dondero had also heard of Gene. At the end of the evening he approached:

"By the way, Gene," he said, "I want you to come down and see me Monday morning."

"What for?" answered Gene.

Dondero got right to the point. "I want to hire you."

Although flattered, Gene did not take the offer seriously.

"Mr. Dondero," he answered, "I appreciate your offer very much, but my life is totally dedicated to teaching. I want to teach. I want to coach. Football has been a big part of my life, and I like it. I think I can be a good football coach. Teaching and coaching are what I went to school for and that's what I want to do."

"I understand," replied Dondero. "But give me the courtesy of coming to see me anyway. Listen to what I have to say."

Reasoning that it could do no harm, Gene agreed and the following Monday morning found himself in Dondero's spacious corner office at the creamery. The wily manager minced no words.

"Gene," he said, "I need a man like you as a field man to go around to farmers in the area and buy milk. You grew up here; people know you and you are well liked. You speak Italian and can communicate with the Italian dairymen. You'd be a natural."

Dondero went on to explain that he would triple whatever Gene was making at the JC and would also provide a company car and expenses. Incredibly, Gene declined.

"I still told him no," recalled Gene. "I just felt that coaching and teaching was what I was cut out to do."

But Dondero wouldn't give in. "Look," he advised. "Ask around. Check me out. Consult your friends and those you trust. After you've sought their advice, make your decision. Either way, it won't hurt our relationship."

It was reasonable advice. Gene agreed.

"In truth, even though it was a great offer, I had no intention of taking it," said Gene. "But I followed his advice. I talked to John Watson, a prominent agriculturist in the area. I talked to Dick Blewett and Dr. Floyd Bailey, president at the JC. They all told me I'd be nuts not to take it. I talked to Evie of course; she said to do whatever I wanted. I know it seems ridiculous, but it was a tough decision for me."

"Anyway," he continued, "coach Blewett and Dr. Bailey told me that teaching and coaching were always there for me if it didn't work out. I figured I had one child, and by that time, Evie was expecting Bonnie. I was only making about $2,000 a year. I knew we could sure use the money. So I thought about it and finally by the next week I went and saw George and accepted his offer."

But there was one proviso.

"I told him I'd take the job on one condition," said Gene. I told him that I wanted to keep my hands in football. There were a lot of kids coming back from the service whose lives had been interrupted by the war and wanted to play ball. I explained that I wanted to keep my name associated with coaching just in case the new job didn't work out. I wanted to start a town team. I told him we'd practice two nights a week and play on weekends so it wouldn't interfere with work."

Ever the sports fan, Dondero agreed. "I'd like to help," he offered. "How much money do you need to start your team?"

"None," answered Gene. "We'll do it on our own."

THE LEGHORNS

Gene as coach of the Leghorns.

XXXIII

"Gene was Petaluma's equivalent to Vince Lombardi. He could have been mayor!"

Newspaper columnist and Peopleologist, Bill Soberanes

By the mid-1950's America was flourishing. Thanks to the GI Bill, millions of returned veterans had earned college degrees, were working in a thriving economy and raising families in cookie-cutter housing tracts purchased with loans provided by the Veteran's Administration. The baby boom was in full flower and a startling new device called television was helping to re-shape the nation's sociology.

But none of this happened overnight. In fact, in some respects the five years immediately following the war resembled the ones that had preceded it. This was especially true in the world of professional football.

Being paid to play football was nothing new. Indeed the practice had been around (legally or otherwise) since 1892 when the Allegheny Athletic Association paid Yale University's all America guard, William W. "Pudge" Heffelfinger, the grand sum of $500 for his services in a game against the Pittsburgh Athletic

Club. But in general, taking money to play what was considered an amateur sport was considered vulgar and unacceptable.

But in 1920 a group of enterprising men (including a former Rose Bowl MVP and New York Yankee outfielder named George S. Halas) met in the empty showroom of Ralph E. Hays' Hupmobile dealership in Canton, Ohio. By the end of the evening Halas's team, the Staley's (so called because they were sponsored by the Staley Starch Works of Decatur, Illinois) was part of a new four team league (three more joined shortly thereafter) called the American Professional Football Conference. A year later the league changed its name to the National Football League (NFL) and professional football was on its way.

The venture was precariously successful. Money was tight, fans were few and recognition was sparse. Nonetheless the fledgling league managed to stay in business throughout WWII, albeit as a plebian second cousin to the vastly more popular (and socially acceptable) college game.

As the end of the war drew near a new league called the All-American Football Conference (AAFC) challenged the NFL by vying for the services of the many talented players coming home from the war. Rocco Pirro was among them and he and his wife Ida's experience typify the life of a pro footballer in that era.

"For the last two years of the war Rock and I lived in Pleasanton in the Bay area," Ida recalled. "Rock was playing service ball for the Fleet City Blue Jackets. When the war ended, he took a $500 bonus to jump from the NFL (where he'd played with Pittsburgh before the war) to play for the Buffalo Bison's (later the Bills) in the new AAFC."

"Pro football was not at all what it is today," she continued. "It was all very local. Without TV most people did not know any players or ever saw a game. Even newspaper coverage was scant. Local papers recognized their own but you had to be a real sports fanatic to know about pro footballers. Some teams drew well, but one could not compare it to college."

Hence, despite the fact that the two professional leagues had teams on both coasts (the San Francisco 49'er's were in the AAFC), without the catalyst of television exposure the game remained a provincial attraction. There was little that was All-American or National about professional football.

Santa Rosa JC Coach's Dick Blewett and Gene Benedetti.. Circa 1945

As a result, towns all over America formed their own teams. Called semi-pro, or club teams, they were a hybrid that fell somewhere between the colleges and the full time professionals. Organization at the semi-pro level varied, as did the quality of play. Rosters were fluid and it was not uncommon for college players to pick up a few bucks playing a little Sunday ball under assumed names. Even Rocco Pirro - under a dubious Greek cognomen - played for pay when he attended Catholic University.

"He got fifty dollars a game," laughed Ida, "until his helmet got knocked off and a sportswriter recognized him. That was the end of his moonlighting."

It was in this pre-television window of time that Gene started a team in Petaluma.

"We called ourselves the Leghorns," he said, "to honor Petaluma's ties to the poultry industry. Our success was purely happenstance. The timing was perfect. It was right after the war and people were starved for entertainment. There was no TV and

The 1949 Leghorns: Front row L to R: Ray Moneymaker, Don Rudolphi, Bill Dorsett, Ed "Short Arms" Webb, Ernie Altenruther, Butch Burtner, Bill Moore, Ken McNutly (QB), Bob Acrone (#2), Stan "Bebe" Mohr (#7), Bill Spaletta (#13).

no one wanted to go all the way to San Francisco to watch a game. We had a captive audience."

Unlike many minor league teams of the day, the Leghorns were exceedingly well organized. Gene was the head coach, local insurance broker and former high school coach George Norwood was appointed business manager, Bob Acrone (who was still playing) assumed the role of team publicist, and Shorty Welch handled the equipment.

To test public reaction, the team borrowed uniforms from the high school and played a single game in 1946. "We played the USF JV squad on Armistice Day," Gene said. "They were coached by my old friend from college, Doc Haley. I had no idea if anyone would even show up to watch us. But the fans came out in droves and filled the stadium."

Confident that his idea was sound, Gene scheduled an eleven game season for 1947.

"Now, you have to remember," he laughed at the memory. "We had no money. So we went down to Milners sporting goods

A Sunset Athletic Club ball carrier pursued by the Leggies. Check out the old fashioined cross-body block.

("where sportsmen serve sportsmen") on Kentucky Street to buy uniforms and equipment for thirty-three players."

It was a moment only Gene could have pulled off.

"Sure Gene," said the proprietor. "I'd love to sell you uniforms and equipment for your new team. Who's going to pay?"

"No problem," Gene answered suavely. "No problem at all. Why my good friend George Norwood here will co-sign, and so will my old pal Bob Acrone - right guys?"

"It was really funny," laughed Gene. "We didn't have a dime between us. But I told the guy that we were good for it. He knew we'd drawn a great crowd for our one game the year before. He knew we'd pay him. He was a good guy. Not many business owners would sell that much equipment on the come."

It is an understatement to call the Leghorns a success. They were a phenomenon. After starting the 1947 season with seven sell-out victories – one of them on Armistice Day before an enormous throng of 7,000 at Santa Rosa's Bailey Field, and another, a 77-0 rout over the hated Santa Rosa Bonecrushers, Gene's classy boys in blue and gold that fans had lovingly christened the "Leggies" acquired the trappings of a civic religion.

One of the few times the Leggies left town was for the 1949 Furit Bowl in Kezar against the Oakland Blue Devils. Here George Legorio hauls in a pass from Fred "The Fox" Klemenok for a sizable gain.

The team was supported by the entire community. Nearly every prominent business advertised in game programs. Gilardi's Tavern (on Washington Street where the Bank of America currently resides) became the unofficial team headquarters. Each week Mooch Lucchesi's L&L barber shop (a three-chair tonsorial that specialized in Butches and Slitzies) hung a gallery of photographs from the previous week's action for patrons to peruse while they waited for a chair. Gene's brother-in-law Red Libarle, proprietor of the Lace House

Laundry, cleaned the team's uniforms for free. The club even sold season tickets.

"The season tickets were a good deal for everyone," Gene explained. "Regular admission was a dollar per game. A season ticket was seven dollars so the buyer saved a few bucks. We did so well with season tickets that we paid for our equipment and insurance and all of our miscellaneous expenses before the season even started. From the first game on it was all gravy."

With overflow crowds, playing the Leggies was a profitable venture for visiting teams.

"We seldom if ever left town," said Gene. "We didn't have to. After the first few games, everyone wanted to come up to our place to play. They made more money that way. Hell, they played at home in front of 400. When they came up here they played in front of 4,000 and got a guaranteed cut of the gate. Why would they want to stay home?"

It was also a good deal for the players.

"We ran it like a business," said Gene. "We bought accident insurance for the players, who were all working men with families, so they'd be covered if they got hurt. We practiced on Tuesday and Thursday nights. Every Thursday after practice we'd go down to the Coca-Cola plant and meet in their conference room. George Norwood would deliver a financial report on the game receipts of the week before. He'd hold back whatever was needed for operating expenses. Then we'd split the rest into equal shares and pay the players. We always referred to the money as "expenses" so as not to jeopardize anyone's eligibility if they returned to school to play."

In an era where the average worker made about $2500 a year, playing for the Leggies was big time.

"We paid pretty well," Gene confirmed. "Each guy got between thirty and forty bucks a week. That was good money in those days."

For the kids in town the Leggies were life itself. Paul Halvorson was twelve years old when his family moved to Petaluma in 1948.

"We lived on Sonoma Avenue a few doors up from North Fair Street," he recalled. "My best buddies were Phil Talamantes, Leroy Bean, Roger Sanborn and Frank Raney. We all lived within a few doors of each other at the corner of North Fair and Sonoma. The street sign said No. Fair so we called ourselves the "No Fair Gang" after the street sign. We were inseparable."

"The Leghorns were our entire lives," Paul went on. "I never knew one person who did not go to the Leggie game every week. It cost $.50 for kids but we always hopped the fence. Later Roger became manager of the school track team and had a key so he'd let our whole gang in through the gate. The crowds were huge and the players were our heroes. Fred "The Fox" Klemonok, "Texas Jack" Moore, and of course Roger's Uncle, Eddie "Short Arms" Webb - he kicked the final extra point when the Leggies pounded some team 101-0!"

"As far as we knew all the players worked at the creamery for Coach Benedetti," continued Halvorson. "I used to ride my bike past the co-op on my way to work at my dad's auto parts store. I'd always look in the window and try to catch a glimpse of Mr. Benedetti. To me, he was like Vince Lombardi. He was bigger than life."

"Petaluma was just a wonderful place for a kid to grow up in those years," he concluded. "And the Leggies were a fantastic experience for every kid in town."

Faces of the 1949 Egg Bowl - top L to R: Fred "The Fox" Klemenok, Ray Moneymaker running for a touchdown, Al Pisenti running down an opponent. Bottom left: Ira Blue of KGO and Curley Acrone, The Leggie faithful and George Legorio, Egg Bowl Queen, Mickey Myles.

Faces of the Leggies. Clockwise from bottom left: Ray Moneymaker, George Legorio, Al Pisenti and Gene's life long friend and Egg Bowl Founder, Butch Burtner.

It was a tough brand of football

Levitcus and the Leggie Faithful.

As the team continued winning it gained wider notoriety due in large part to the efforts of Bob Acrone. Acrone, who owned the Union Oil service station in town and still starred on the team, was also a talented public relations man. Writing under the improbable by-line "LEG-HORN" in the local papers, he made sure that every aspect of Leggie information was published in the press. In 1949 the team was the highest scoring machine in the nation and national papers like the *San Francisco Chronicle* ran stories on the gridiron power in the little town north of the Bay.

Acrone's efforts were augmented by another Petalumian named Ira Blue. A die-hard Leggie fan, Blue was the sports editor at KGO, a major radio station in San Francisco.

"Ira loved the Leggies," said Gene. "He'd broadcast our scores each week and extol our virtues on KGO. Millions of people in the bay area knew about the Leghorns, even though they'd never been to Petaluma."

The team was special in ways beyond the gridiron. June Burtner (Petaluma High School class of 1938) remembers:

"The Leghorns were wonderful," she said fondly. "My husband Butch had played with Gene in high school and later down at USF. They were lifelong friends. When the war came, Butch went into the Army. He served in the Pacific under horrendous conditions. His situation was typical of many boys on the team. When they got back from the war there was no place for them to go to talk about their experiences - to be together with others who understood. I remember Butch speaking about how it was great to be among his friends and to have an outlet. In that regard the Leghorns were very therapeutic."

"Butch was a wonderful guy and a great husband and father," June went on. "He had a wonderful smile. He loved his town and his friends. It was Butch who started the Egg Bowl."

Burtner's idea was typical of the civic pride held by Gene and all the men on the team.

"Butch was a great guy," remembered Gene. "He was very community minded. He got the idea of playing a game for charity. So we decided to play the last game of the year and donate all the proceeds. We called the game the Egg Bowl and it went pretty well."

It did indeed. In fact, the Egg Bowl became a signature event. Each year the players as well as shopkeepers sold advance tickets. An Egg Bowl Queen and her court were crowned to ride in the Egg Bowl Parade and preside over half-time festivities. After the game both teams and their guests were feted at a gala dinner dance at one of the towns hotels - either the Petaluma or the Yosemite.

"It was a great occasion every year," said Gene. "We formed an Egg Bowl Committee and disbursed the proceeds to various charities. It was our way of saying thanks to our town."

Despite the public adulation, the Leghorns remained an intimate team. Gene's nephew Dan Libarle remembers:

"I was the water boy," he said. "I was about ten years old. I remember the games of course, but the thing that sticks in my mind was going over to my uncle Shorty (his name for Gene) and aunt Evie's house on the mornings before the games. All of the players would show up. One by one they'd hop up on aunt Evie's kitchen table and Uncle Shorty would tape their ankles. He never let anyone else touch his players. They were like his sons and he taped each guy himself. While the players were waiting to be taped, aunt Evie would cook sweet rolls for them and she'd also put them to work doing chores around the house.

"Dan's right," confirmed former Leggie lineman Fran Burke. "Gene and Evelyn's house was pretty small and there'd be a dozen or so guys over getting taped. Evelyn was just a wonderful woman. She was just so gracious. She made us all feel like family."

In 1947 Don Ramataci (who would one day coach the Leghorns and become a successful insurance broker) was a nineteen-year-old college drop-out.

"I played my freshman year at USF in 1946," said Ramataci. "The next year I stayed home and played for the Leggies. It was really something. Gene was a great coach. He had a great football mind. But his greatest attribute was his leadership. We'd do anything for him. If he told us to jump in the river, we'd have done it. Every man on the team felt the same way. After I played that first year, Gene told me to get my ass back in school. I really didn't want to go back but he drove me down to The City, talked to the coach at USF and put me back in school. I ended up playing at USF for three more years and graduating. Gene was very instrumental in my doing so. But I'll never forget playing for the Leghorns."

So how good were the Leghorns?

"Realistically, we were a very good semi-pro club," said Ramataci. "We only practiced two nights a week, and we all worked full-time jobs. So it's tough to compare us with a college team. We could have beaten most JC teams, and probably some small colleges. But the brand of ball was plenty tough – it was all you wanted."

Possibly the most peripatetic Leghorn, was Bud Chadwick. A local boy from Cotati, Chadwick's two seasons (1949 and 1950) with the Leggies were part of a twelve year career that saw him play with St. Mary's College, the U.S. Army (both at Fort Ord and in Korea), Cal-Poly San Luis Obispo and the Saskatchewan Rough Riders of the Canadian Football League.

"I agree with Don," said Chadwick. "It was a tough level of semi-pro ball. The competition varied. A few of the teams that came to town were very weak. But most were not. And some were very strong. When good teams came in we played them very tough and beat them. I'd say we were the best semi-pro team on the coast."

"Gene was a fine coach," Bud continued. "Some of his players were the same age as he, but he had a wonderful rapport with everyone. He made us want to do anything for him. If he told us to, we'd have lined up against anybody."

While organization, civic pride, philanthropy, team loyalty and leadership were all essential parts of the Leghorn's success, the foundation of the club was its fans. Indeed, it would be difficult to imagine a more enthusiastic, and eccentric lot than the droves of Petalumians that squeezed into Durst Field (which was expanded each year to accommodate them) to cheer for the Leggies.

"The whole town emptied out on game day," recalled Fran Burke. "You could have shot a cannon down Kentucky Street and not hit a soul."

Dressed in Leggie Blue and Gold, they descended on Durst Field like a wild hoard and roared from the moment the gates opened until the final gun. Sometime during the first year, a crazed Leggiephile brought a live Leghorn rooster to the game. The fans named him Leviticus. Trained to crow on cue, the screeching bird was passed up and down the aisles and held proudly aloft when the Leggies did anything good on the field. If Leviticus didn't feel like crowing, local wag Al Herman took his place. Between the churning sea of Blue and Gold, the never ending din of noise and the howls of Leviticus and Herman, playing in "Leggie Land" defined home field advantage.

And it wasn't just the fans. In the early years, one of Gene's best friends Doc Haley often served as referee. And the town's Justice of the Peace, Rollie Webb, was the line judge.

"Old Rollie," laughed Bud Chadwick. "Lord, what a character. He was the local Justice of the Peace. He had his own private code of justice. I don't think there was a kid in town that did not appear before him at one time or another. When I was in high school, I ran the town's only stop sign. I had to go in front of Judge Webb. He asked me how much money I had. When I told him I was broke, he ordered me to write a two hundred-word essay on the dangers of running a stop sign. Now there's something you'd never see today!"

Apparently, Judge Webb's sense of justice extended beyond the bench to the Leghorn sidelines.

"The Honorable Judge Rollie," laughed Gene. "God bless him. He ran the down markers and was in charge of the chain gang. He also liked to have a nip or two before the game (or just about anytime for that matter). I remember a number of times we'd run a play and I'd say to myself, 'we're short of the first down,' old Rollie would come rumbling out, measure the gain and signal first down."

Ramataci agreed: "Let's just say he could stretch the down marker when we needed it," he chuckled.

Petaluma's official storyteller was Bill Soberanes. In a career that spanned nearly fifty years, Bill wrote 13,000 consecutive columns for the *Argus-Courier* and never missed a deadline. The founder of the World Wrist Wrestling Championships, Bill was the quintessential Peopleologist to generations of Petalumians as he strolled around town smoking his pipe and sharing fellowship and stories with his many friends. In a 2003 interview a few weeks before his death, the man who Gene credits with "making the Leghorns famous" shared his memories.

"There are many things that come to mind about the Leghorns," he grinned. "Of course there were the fans. And then there were the many teams that came to play, the South San Francisco Windbreakers, the Piedmont Buds, the Oakland Devils (an all African-American team that we played at Kezar in the 1949 Fruit Bowl), the Richmond Wolfpack and of course the Santa Rosa Bonecrushers. But the one I remember most was Horsetrader Ed's San Francisco Broncos. What a day that was!"

Edward R. Shapiro was "Horsetrader Ed." Dealing in "used motor cars" from his car lots in the bay area the Horsetrader was an early edition of today's insufferable car dealers who advertise on television. A combination of entrepreneur, huckster, ringmaster and slickeroo, the Horsetrader was also a dedicated sportsman and avid football fan. In 1950, he put together a powerful semi-pro team stocked with former college players and even a few pros.

"The old Horsetrader himself came up to see me," laughed Gene. He was quite a guy. A good guy really. He asked me if he could come up and play in the 1950 Egg Bowl. I knew he would be a big draw and he had a great team so I told him to come on up. I promised him a guarantee and a cut of the gate. He wanted a written contract. I told him no, that my word was good. Then he wanted to know if he could bring his horse. I didn't know why he needed a horse, but told him to go ahead and bring it. Hell, I didn't care."

"It was really great," laughed Soberanes. "It was a beautiful day. They'd had a big parade for the Egg Queen and her court. The stands were filled with cheering fans. The sky was blue and the whole town gleamed against the backdrop of our mountains.

All of a sudden out rides the Horsetrader dressed up like a cowboy shooting his six-shooters into the air. The fans went wild. It is my fondest Leghorn memory."

After five years, with a sparkling record of forty wins, six losses and one tie, Gene retired from the Leghorns. In a heartfelt display of appreciation the Leggie faithful gave he and the family a "Benedetti Night." It was a grand event as Evelyn, lovely in a long fur coat, dressed the four kids, Michelle, Bonnie, Donna and little Danny in their Sunday best and took them to the game. Gene's parents Giacondo and Pia were there as well. The fans showered the family with an array of gifts including a dining room set, and a television. In the floodlit stadium the family stood together in the brisk autumn night and waved to the crowd. Someone snapped a picture and caught a moment in time when a great ball club and a beloved coach brought a deep sense of community pride to the little town in Sonoma valley in the roseate years before America was big.

Benedetti Night. Giacondo and Pia, Jack Dei, Gene, Evie, Michelle, Bonnie, Donna and little Danny (looking very dapper in his hat and little white shoes.)

CLOVER COUNTRY

"Even the founders would not have imagined the modern processing and bottling plant.."

XXXIV

"Aren't you glad you live in Clover Country?"
Early Petaluma Co-op advertising slogan.

1963 marked the fiftieth anniversary of the Petaluma Co-operative Creamery. Things had come a long way. Even its visionary founders would have marveled at the glistening white bottling and processing plant with its fleet of sleek delivery trucks that now occupied the once dusty lot at Western and Baker streets. By now Gene had served the creamery for seventeen years and had long since replaced George Dondero as General Manager.

"When I first started all I knew about the dairy business was how to milk a cow," said Gene. "But George was a great mentor. He started me on the road as a field man. My job was to go around and buy milk from the local farmers. There was a lot to learn. If they had complaints or problems, I had to have an answer. If there was something I didn't know, I'd promise to get back to them the next day. Every afternoon at 4:00 pm, I'd go back to the office and George and I would review the entire day. He'd evaluate each call. That's how I learned. After a year or so he hired my replacement and had me train him. Then I moved inside."

For over a decade after its inception the sole product of the creamery was butter, almost all of which was shipped in bulk to San Francisco. In the 1920's a seasonal need for milk developed among the resorts on the Russian River that grew into a small home delivery market in Petaluma. After World War Two, the population boom along with the availability of the household refrigerator (by 1950 90% of American had one) expanded the home delivery market even more. By the mid-1950's the trod of the Clover man (the company had adopted the brand name in 1939) and the clink of milk bottles was as familiar a sound on North Bay front porches as the flop of the morning paper.

To meet these increasing needs the creamery expanded accordingly and organized its facilities into two production lines; one for fluid products, milk and cream, and the other for manufactured products; butter, sour cream, cottage cheese, and later, powdered milk. Mastering the complexities of what was now a cutting edge manufacturing and bottling operation required a comprehensive on-the-job curriculum. George Dondero started Gene at the beginning.

"George started me in receiving," Gene said, "where the milk was brought in right off the farms. That's when I really started learning the guts of the business."

The work in receiving was tough and unglamorous. Each ten-gallon can, some weighing up to one hundred pounds and marked with a number corresponding to the dairy from which it came, was unloaded by hand and weighed on a large scale. After popping off the top with a rubber mallet, a sample was taken to the laboratory to be incubated and tested for butterfat and impurities. The contents were then dumped into huge holding tanks and thence into industrial-sized centrifuges. When the centrifuges were set a-spinning the raw milk separated into cream and skim milk, each draining into separate vats. Both products were then pasteurized (heated to a specified temperature to destroy harmful bacteria) and standardized (a process that added appropriate levels of fats and solids). Grade A milk (that of the highest quality) was bottled as fluids. The lesser grades were manufactured into non-fluid products.

"That receiving room was tough work," said Gene. "Those cans were heavy. But it was good to work with the guys out there and get to know them."

After a few months in receiving, Gene continued his education in the manufacturing area, the heart of which was the butter room. Here the huge vats of pasteurized cream were dumped into enormous churns that looked like giant misshapen cement mixers. After adding a little salt (for flavor and to retard bacterial spoilage) and annatto (a dye derived from the annatto seed to give the butter its soft yellow color) the churns were activated. The ensuing din – which sounded like a line of unbalanced washing machines run amok - reached its crescendo when the fat globules in the cream congealed and "threw the butter." When the cycle was finished, workmen removed the soft butter by hand and packaged it in sixty-eight pound boxes lined with seepage resistant parchment paper. The excess liquid, (buttermilk) was drained off and either bottled or used for other products.

Gene also learned the bottling operation – a part of the company that was undergoing significant change. In the early years, all milk was bottled in glass. But by the mid-1940's a new technology developed by the American Can Company (Cannco) had perfected the wax-lined paper carton. Rectangular with a square top, the Cannco container was limited to quarts, pints and

½ pints and featured a corner tab that allowed the user to conveniently pour the contents. Indeed, many is the child of the 50's who recalls opening a ½ pint of milk at the school lunch table, ripping off the little tab to prevent getting a white dollop on his nose and taking a cold swig.

A few years later the Ex-Cell-O Corporation (a Detroit company that manufactured precision production tools) acquired distribution rights to the American Paper Bottle Companies patented Pure-Pak system and took bottling to the next level by perfecting the gable-top carton with a folding spout. Still in use today, the design could accommodate all carton sizes and changed the industry. Because paper cartons were single service and did not need to be returned, dairies could now ship liquid products to wider geographic areas. Moreover, carton stock was shipped flat and saved storage and shipping costs.

"The paper carton changed everything," said Gene. "Glass had been a real hassle. It was heavy and difficult to handle and there was always breakage. It was also very labor intensive. Each day the drivers would return with thousands of dirty bottles. We had a big bottle washing operation to clean and sterilize them. It was all a lot of work and cost us a fortune. But with the Pure-Pak line we could bottle and deliver all of our liquids in the gable top carton that you still see today. We had the first Pure-Pak bottling line in Northern California and it saved us a ton of expense."

But there was also a down side.

"With the traditional glass bottles," explained Gene, "the consumer could see the product, especially the cream that had risen to the top. It was called the cream plug. Housewives would scoop it out with a spoon and use it for coffee or whipped cream or whatever. If you wanted to mix the milk you just shook the bottle. Seeing clean milk with a cream plug was a sign of quality and was used as a marketing tool. So when cartons came in, it was a problem because the housewife could no longer see the milk or the cream plug."

The answer was homogenization; a process where milk is heated and strained under pressure forcing the fat globules to separate to the point where they cannot re-congeal, thereby preventing the formation of a cream plug.

"People think that homogenization is just for mixing the milk," Gene said. "But that's only part of the reason. A primary reason for the process is purely cosmetic and was brought about by the fact that cartons prevented the customer from seeing the milk."

After gaining a working knowledge of all aspects of the physical plant and the in-office and business procedures, Gene was summoned to see George Dondero.

Gene," he said. "You're ready to start taking on bigger responsibilities. I'd like to have you take my place someday and in order for you to move to that level, I need all of your attention. You've got to make a decision about football."

"That's when I retired from the Leghorns," said Gene. "George was very active in the community and the industry. It was part of his job. At one time or another, he had served as Director or President of all the industry associations. He explained that he wanted me to start going to meetings with him so that I could get to know the other people in the state. He always took his wife along and wanted me to take Evie. That's when I started to travel and really gain a presence in the industry and to learn the business from that level. In 1955, George was promoted to Assistant to the President of the board and I took over as General Manager. He had been a great teacher. He was one of the most intelligent men I ever knew. The education he gave me was better than anything I could have ever acquired in college. George Dondero is the man who gave me a chance and got me ready. I owe him a great deal."

FAMILY

A family of the 50's.

XXXV

"We always waited for Dad to come home for dinner.
We always ate together …
a full rich meal that Mom cooked … "

Donna Benedetti

The Benedetti kids were children of the fifties. Theirs was a world as crisp and clean as the crew cuts, salt and pepper cords, and plaid jumpers they wore to St. Vincent's Catholic school. Like the black and white TV shows of Bonanza and the Mickey Mouse Club, their lives were simple and defined. By the time they came of age almost everything had changed.

In 1956 they watched the Ed Sullivan Show and heard a gravel poor teenager from Tupelo Mississippi belt out "Hound Dog" in a pulsating beat culled from the cotton rows of the Deep South. Eight years later, they watched again as four shaggy-haired English boys from the Mersey River clubs of Liverpool captured America's youth with "I Want To Hold Your Hand."

When oldest daughter Michelle entered the University of California at Berkeley in 1961, college students went to hootenannies, hung out in smoke- filled coffeehouses and listened to Peter, Paul and Mary. The drug of choice was beer and everyone wondered what they were going to do when they got out of school. A few years later, when eldest son Dan entered Sonoma State College, kids tripped to Carlos Santana, swayed to the soulful blues of Janis Joplin, and grooved to the riffs of Jimi Hendrix's blazing white Stratocaster. For them, the drugs of choice were many, and young men wondered how to best handle the looming specter of the draft. In the spring of 1967, a blue eyed tenor named Scott McKenzie sang a gentle anthem at a gathering called the Monterey Pop Festival. And later that summer, thousands of youngsters put a flower in their hair and flocked to San Francisco for the Summer of Love.

From an early Christmas card.

In the years when Gene's kids were growing up, the nation saw a plain spoken Missourian, a revered war hero from Kansas, a blue-blood patrician from Massachusetts, a tall powerful Texan and a small town Californian serve as President.

For Americans it was an era of unparalleled triumph and heartbreaking tragedy. We reached for the stars and put a man on the moon. But we also lost 36,000 of our sons in a bloody (and all but forgotten) war in Korea, and another 58,000 in the hot and horrible jungles of Vietnam. And when murderous snipers killed our President in Dallas, and shot down a courageous and peaceful preacher on a hotel balcony in Memphis, our national innocence was lost forever.

When the Benedetti kids were children, most young Americans didn't know enough about their government to distrust it. By the time they were young adults, there was enough national angst to almost tear it asunder.

In the midst of all this, Gene and Evelyn loved each other, reared six children, lived in three different homes and gathered their family each evening for supper.

"When we were kids," said Gene's daughter Donna," we always waited for Dad to come home from work. He worked a lot, and was often late. But we always waited for him. I remember watching the Mickey Mouse Club around 5:00 pm. Dad would come home and he and Mom would have a drink together and a few moments by themselves. Then we'd all sit at the table and eat dinner. The evening meal was very important. It was our family time and Mom always made a full rich meal for us to enjoy."

This looks like a scene from "Father Knows Best". The TV was a gift from the Leggie fans from Benedetti Night.

Three different houses hold memories for the family.

"We started out on 5th street," remembered oldest son Dan of the little Spanish stucco dwelling. "But we outgrew it pretty fast. When mom and dad first moved there they just had Michelle. But over a three year period Bonnie, Donna and I were born one right after the other. Our backyard backed up to Petaluma General Hospital. The running joke was that Dad had moved there so that if mom was going to have a baby all she had to do was jump over the fence into the maternity ward. Shortly after I was born, we moved."

"After Dan came along I had a chance to buy some land on the edge of town," said Gene. "In those days you could get a parcel for a good price and since it was out in the country it was a good deal. It was located on a dirt lane called West Street. My old friend Colin Holmes bought a parcel across the valley and built a home too."

The new house was bigger both inside and out. Colin Holmes' daughter, Lynn Holmes-Imm remembers: "We lived on Shuman Road, across this little green valley from the Benedetti's," she laughed. "Today the area is all housing tracts. But when we were kids, it was all country. The Benedetti's had a big Doberman pincher dog. His name was Aaron. He used to scare me when I'd go out to ride my horse. Those two guys, Gene and my dad, they were really something."

"They were all of that," agreed Dan. "The two houses were close enough that Dad and Colin used to stand in their back yards and hit golf balls across the valley at each other. Colin would slam one over and Dad would blast it back. They even built a little golf course between the houses. They were like a couple of kids!"

But it wasn't just Gene and Colin.

"My mother, Dottie and Evie were best friends," laughed Lynn. "Together they were like an ongoing 'I Love Lucy' skit. One time they got the idea that their refrigerators needed to be painted. Evie had read in some magazine that you could fill a vacuum cleaner with paint and use it as a spray painter. So they went down to the local appliance store and asked the guy if it was possible to spray paint with their vacuum cleaners. When he told them it was, they moved the refrigerators out in the garage and filled their vacuum cleaners with paint and turned them on. Naturally it didn't work. What a mess! Mom painted hers gold, and Evie sprayed hers black. It was horrible. The paint didn't stick and it was just a mess. They were looking at each other, covered with paint and saying; 'what are we gonna do?' It was so funny. Gene had to buy Evie a new refrigerator."

The family also took vacations out of town. There were trips to Astero de America – a camping area on the coast between Bodega and Tomales Bay - with their friends the Rattigans and also to Bucks Lake near Quincy, California with the Holmes family.

"I remember those trips," said Lynn. There was a big lodge up there but we stayed in little one-room cabins. It was all very rustic - even for that time. The ice man would come by every morning to fill the old fashioned ice box. All of my parent's friends and their kids would go; the Acrone's, the Klemonok's – all of us were friends."

"At night," she continued, "we'd all go to the lodge for dinner, then we kids would go back to one cabin to sleep together. Our parents would go back to the restaurant to party. They were pretty quiet in the morning. But then mom and Evie would do wash. I still remember them hanging out laundry on clothes-lines. All of the dad's would take us kids fishing and swimming and riding. We were just little kids. Gene and Evie and my mom and dad … they had such a good time together as young parents. It was wonderful."

In 1964, the family moved for a final time.

"I bought two acres from my Dad at the top of the hill on his ranch," explained Gene. "It was my favorite spot when I was a kid. I used to sit under the big tree up there and dream about building a big house. And then I did it."

Evie agreed; "I got to design it," she said. "We built it as a place where we could stay forever – a place with plenty of room for the kids and for us to entertain. I had them make it so it was quiet from room to room. I wanted a big family room with a big fireplace and kitchen. It was really fun to do and I was very excited."

As his family grew so did Gene's presence in the community and his circles of influence.

Joe Rattigan, Cus Pirro's former roommate, had come west after the war and graduated from Stanford Law School. After practicing law for a time in Santa Rosa, Joe became California's youngest state senator and eventually an associate justice on the state court of appeals. One of the Golden State's most prominent legal scholars and orators, Rattigan and his wife Betty became close friends with the Benedetti's.

"Gene was very well known," said Justice Rattigan in 2003. "He was in the very tough and competitive wholesale milk business and was very successful. He was kind of like a godfather to people, and I say that with no negative connotations. He was always trying to help someone and was universally respected. He knew and associated with many prominent people, both locally and in the state and even the national government.

For the kids, Gene's position in the community was a growing awareness and each saw their father's position differently.

"I just remember that Dad worked very hard," said Michelle. "He'd come home for dinner tired and stressed and sometimes grumpy."

"Then, she laughed. " He'd want to know why we were not bright and cheerful."

"When we were little," said Donna, "we were not really aware of his friends. But still, it was a little different for us. Dad served on the Fair Board and we always had free entrée to the rides, which for a little kid was really cool. He also got us front row seats to the annual rodeo, which I hated, but went anyway. In that regard his position was special. As time went on, we began to realize that he knew special people."

"For example," she continued, "George Christopher, the mayor of San Francisco and his wife Tula visited us on a number of occasions. That was a big deal. I mean here was the mayor of San Francisco having a drink with my parents! To me, that was a big deal."

"And of course," she concluded, "there were the Rattigan's. They were our very close friends. Joe was very prominent and powerful."

"I agree," said Bonnie. "We knew that he held a different position in town. And he worked a lot. He'd come home for dinner and then go back to work at night. But yes, as I grew older, I knew he held more than just a regular job."

"When I was young," said Dan, "he was just my Dad. When I played Little League, he was just another father in the stands. I knew he had a lot of friends but thought of him as just a regular father. I didn't become aware of his influence until later. For example, when I was about fourteen years old, there was some kind of union problem at his work. Some nightriders drove up to our house and fired a gunshot into the air. I remember Dad loading up his shotgun and going out to what I think was a union meeting. He was not going to let anyone shove him or his people around. And he sure as hell wasn't going to let anyone come on to his land and threaten or hurt his family."

"In later years," Dan continued, "Dad was involved with Sonoma State University. His friend, State Senator Joe Rattigan had founded the school in 1960. The college was very liberal and Dad felt that it was a little too radical – that it was not what a college should be. He was to Sonoma State what Senator Sam Hayakawa was to San Francisco State. He formed an association called "The friends of Sonoma State" to promote conservative values at the school. There was tremendous adversity surrounding his involvement. The Governor at the time was Ronald Regan. Even though Dad was a democrat, Regan appointed him to the California State University Board of Trustees. Some of Dad's political enemies drove up to our house in the middle of the night and yelled out threats to our family. It scared Mom. But Dad was never afraid of that kind of stuff. He was absolutely fearless when it came to defending his family. He never lacked the courage of his convictions. When those kinds of things happened I realized that his life and work went far beyond his job at the creamery."

"That's true," agreed younger brother Herm. "Dad never backed off of what he believed. We always knew we were Benedetti's. We always had a sense of what that meant. I was always aware that I could not step too far out of line because of who my Dad was."

As the youngest, Gina had her own impression.

"In a lot of ways being the youngest had its advantages," she mused. "I sat at the dinner table every night and watched it all unfold. We had the normal youthful rebellion and believe me I learned from it. Mom and Dad's friends were just part of my life. To me it was no big deal. When someone like Mayor Christopher or Congressman Don Clausen, or State Assemblyman Bill Bagley, or the President of the University, or anybody else came up to the house…hey I wasn't impressed. They were just friends of my parents."

"But I do remember when Bill Walton came over," she grinned. "I didn't know a thing about basketball and could have cared less about it. So in that context I didn't know who he was. But when he had to bend over to step into our front room, (Walton is nearly seven feet tall) now that was something a kid would remember!"

"But," she continued, "by the time I was a teenager I began to realize that Mom and Dad knew a lot of important people. We had a big brass bowl that we put all of the Christmas cards into each year. I recall helping Mom open them and reading who they were from. We'd get them from all over and from all kinds of people. Senators, congressmen, judges, and for years we got one from Ronald and Nancy Regan. I remember being impressed with that."

For the grandkids, it was all a matter of course. Grandson Marcus Benedetti: "One time when I was little – I must have been about nine - I went up to the big house and Sally Ride was there. Of course I knew that she was the first woman astronaut and was totally impressed. She was great and gave me a little patch for my jacket and, as I recall, an autograph. She was really nice. Meeting her was neat, but the fact that she was at the big house was not a big deal. She was just the kind of people that came to see my grandparents."

"But you know," Marcus went on, "my grandfather's friends were just like him. Men like Don Classen and Jim Leprino, and Joe Rattigan. They were all men who came up tough. They were all humble and very unpretentious. They didn't waste food, or flaunt their power or wealth. They were the antithesis of what one would expect of powerful men. It made me proud and confident that my grandparents knew such people."

His connections and influence notwithstanding, Gene's home grown ethos never wavered. He was proud of his heritage and throughout his life continued to celebrate the apotheosis of the ordinary person. For him, a man was judged by his performance, not his papers.

"Both mom and dad treated everyone equally," said Dan. In fact, most of Dad's friends were not big shots. They were people that he grew up with. Men like Stiney and Bob Acrone and Colin Holmes and uncle Red. They were the guys he went to school with, who lived and struggled through the depression and came up tough. He didn't care who you were or what you did. If you were a guest in our house, you were welcome and treated like anyone else. Our parents respected all of their friends and all of our friends. They were gracious to anyone who was in our home."

"That is absolutely true," agreed Bob Acrone. "Gene never changed. He never changed at all. We all took an annual fishing trip. Gene, myself, Stiney, Don Ramatici, Butch Brutner, Ed "short arms" Webb, Red Libarle - all of the guys from our school days – we went every year without fail. As our sons got older, we took them. In fact those of us who are left, we still go - and it's been over fifty years. Now we take our sons and grandsons. Gene always cooks and he is a great cook. But we tell him he can't cook worth a damn and tease the hell out of him. Years ago we started calling him "Doby" after a fat little character on the old Sergeant Bilko TV show named private Doberman. We still tease him, call him "Doby" and tell him he can't cook worth a damn."

In the early years, Gene and Evie kept in contact with the Pirro family.

"I wanted Michelle to know who her father was," said Gene. "I never had a problem with that. Cus was such a fine guy. In the years when her uncle Rock was playing for Buffalo we'd take her down to Kezar Stadium when he'd come to town to play the forty-niners. We'd go with the Rattigan's. After the game, if Rock had time, we'd all go to dinner."

On one occasion, Cus' parents, Thomas and Marian even came west for a visit.

"Oh sure, I remember that," said Dan. "Mrs. Pirro made "cuvadilles" for us. They were little pasta balls with sauce. She put a big sheet on the table and rolled the dough just right. Then she cut it into little pieces and with a little flick of her thumb and finger she folded them into little balls. After she shook off the flower she put them into boiling water and all at once we had pasta. She covered them with sauce. They were delicious."

There was a clear division of responsibility in the family. Gene worked and provided, and Evie ran the show at home.

"When we were kids," said Dan, "Mom was amazing. She took Herm and I to all of our games. She got the girls to their cheerleading and baton practice. She got us to school and made sure we were dressed and combed for church on Sunday. She cooked all the meals, and kept everything organized. I don't know how she did it."

"It was more than just that," went on Gina. "Many times Dad called in the afternoon to tell her that a bunch of people were coming to dinner and 'could she throw something together?' And she did it. She was amazing. Dad would show up with some congressman or business person with their entourage or just a bunch of his pals from work or USF and mom would never miss a beat. The ice bucket would be full, the bar stocked, the table set, a wonderful dinner ready, and she would always look stunning – just stunning. She was an amazingly beautiful and gracious hostess, and she could pull it all together out of thin air!"

Evie was also the kid's confidant and intermediary.

"Let's just say that Dad had his own expectations of how we should behave," laughed Herm. "If you stepped out of line, he didn't hesitate to let you know."

"That's very true," grinned Dan. "In some ways I was as stubborn as he was so I got whacked on more than on occasion. I deserved it, though. He had to do something to get my attention."

The girls were different, though.

"As the youngest I just sat and watched," said Gina. "Mom would never disagree with Dad in front of us. But I know that behind closed doors she interceded on our behalf. She understood girls much better than he did. Between the two of them it was a good balance."

"But Dad was very loving," commented Donna. "He'd come into our rooms in the morning singing 'Good morning to you', open the curtains and wake us up for school. He'd give us all a kiss. And then go off to work. None of us were morning people so we'd close the curtains and go back to sleep for a while, but he was still very loving to us. But yes, mom and dad did balance the load and we all felt secure."

"Yes, it was a good balance," agreed Gene. "Evie was always home for the kids. And that's the way we both wanted it. It was important for them to have someone to talk to when they came home from school. They all trusted her and told her everything - much more than they ever told me. And that was good. She was there for all of them. Evie held our entire home together. We never had a squabble. She was the most wonderful mother and wife a man could have had."

THE WORLD OF CLO

Gene and Clo the Cow.

XXXVI

"Support your local cow; buy Clover milk."

Clo the Cow

By 1971 Petaluma had grown from a town of eight thousand citizens to a bustling community three times that size. By now Gene had been with the creamery for twenty-five years. His name and reputation were firmly entrenched in the California dairy industry and the community at large. The creamery itself was a thriving enterprise and a deep part of Petaluma life. While Gene had helped guide the business in countless areas, there were two notable achievements - one far from the community eye and the other very public - that he considers milestones.

Unlike a normal business the objectives of a cooperative are not necessarily tied to profit.

"The primary purpose of a co-op is to buy and market the member's milk." explained Gary Imm, Chief Executive Officer of Clover-Stornetta Farms. "Profit was not a primary concern. As long as the plant stayed open and continued to buy their milk the producers were, for the most part, satisfied. For them, breaking even was good. They made their money selling their milk to the co-op."

Theoretically, this laissez faire approach worked. As late as the 1950s most of the creamery's producers were small farmers. The average herd size was less than twenty cows with each producing about four gallons a day. But as time went on dairying became increasingly sophisticated and efficient. What had once been a business of ten-gallon can routes was now one of rumbling tanker trucks transporting thousands of gallons of milk to an automated twenty-four hour a day processing and bottling plant. As a result, the co-op found itself with an ever-increasing amount of product, and a need to expand.

"Getting bigger was a good thing," said Gene, "but it created a need to upgrade our facilities. To do that, we needed to borrow money. But when we went to the bank we discovered that we didn't have enough equity to qualify for a loan."

The problem lay in the archaic way shares were purchased by the co-op's producers.

"Every year on the 1st of April," Gene explained, "the producers counted the number of cows they were milking. They had to buy one share in the co-op for each cow they were milking on that day. If a guy had fifteen cows, he bought fifteen shares and so on. The problem was you had to take the guy at his word. The next week, that same guy could miraculously be milking twenty-five cows, but had only purchased fifteen shares. Even so we still had to buy and process his milk. In short, people could easily cheat and there was nothing you could do. That system may have worked in the old days but this was modern times. Like any business we needed bank financing. And without a stable equity base no bank would give us a loan. I couldn't blame the bank, their hands were tied. The system we had was very unfair. We needed to change it. The problem was clear to me, but the solution was not."

"I knew something had to be done," he went on. "So I called the University of California at Davis. They had, and still have, one of the top agricultural schools in the nation. A wonderful woman named Alice Jewett-Lowry worked there. She was an expert in the business aspects of agriculture. When I explained our problem she agreed that our system was not only unfair but was also inefficient from a business standpoint. She explained the concept of the "revolving fund.""

Lowry-Jewett's concept was as brilliant as it was revolutionary. Since fat content - which determines the classification (grade 'A' 'B' and so on) of milk and thus its market value - could be measured when incoming loads were tested, it was possible to accurately calculate the quality of each farmer's milk. Lowry-Jewett proposed collecting an annual sum of money from each dairyman based on the fat content of his product. Such a system, she explained would enable each producer to contribute his fair share. The creamery would retain this money and use it for operating capital. After a designated period of time (usually seven years) the money from the first year (called a "retain") would be returned to the dairyman. Since the producer contributed money every year he had a constant balance revolving in his account, a percentage of which was being returned to him each year.

With Lowry-Jewett's revolving fund the business would have access to a consistent pool of operating capital as well as a stable equity base with which to collateralize any required loans. It also gave each producer an incentive to make the best milk possible so the business would be profitable and thus able to return their "retain." In retrospect it seems simple. But at the time, the revolving fund was a radical departure.

""I though it was a hell of an idea," said Gene." So I took it to George Dondero who by this time was the Assistant to the President of the Board. He was not optimistic. You have to understand. The producers were the actual owners of the business. They had to approve what we did. So instead of trying to sell them on the idea myself, I asked Mrs. Lowry-Jewett to come over and talk at a series of meetings. She talked to our board of directors and then we scheduled meetings for all of our members. She was an expert and a very brilliant woman. After she got done talking to them they bought off on the concept."

With each producer now having a vested interest in the growth and profitability of the business the results were dramatic.

"The establishment of the revolving fund changed everything," said Gene "It enabled us to really grow with the times. We had strong brand recognition with the Clover label. Now we could aggressively market our products and expand. We had a source of working capital that was stable and a growing equity. Installing the revolving fund was a major accomplishment in my time at the co-op."

But there was another achievement that, while less complicated, was arguably as notable and imminently more fun.

****

To drive north from San Francisco through the Waldo Tunnel – with its portals painted with rainbows, is to pass from the hustle of the city into a quiet verdure of green pastures, leafy vineyards and endless blue skies. Eclectic and affluent, the five counties,

Marin, Sonoma, Napa, Lake and Mendocino that grace the region are considered by many as California's most lovely. They are also the heart of Clover Country and the domain of a chubby little Holstein named Clo the Cow.

First Clover billboard, 1969.

Early billboard wecoming travelers to Clover Country.

Clo was conceived in the mind of Lee Levinger. A talented ad man, Levinger had handled the creamery's advertising account since 1951. It was he who came up with the signature slogan,

"Aren't you glad you live in Clover country?" Throughout the fifties and sixties, Levinger's ads focused on Clover Country's natural beauty and the family values inherent in its rural culture. Under Levinger there were even a series of TV ads featuring one day CEO Gary Imm with his wife Lynn and their two small sons frolicking in the green fields. But Levinger was more than just an ad man. He was an instinctive visionary.

"Lee was such a great guy," Gene recalled fondly. "He and I used to go to lunch and have a martini or two and shake dice and talk business. He was a brilliant man who really understood people. He had an uncanny sense – just a gut feeling - for what caught people's attention and what made them buy."

"Lee came up with the idea for Clo. We were having lunch one day in 1969 and he showed me a drawing of a caricature of a cow. He said it was just a concept, and that he wanted to put in on a billboard. I told him he was nuts. Our area is very environmentally sensitive. At the time, Marin County had just passed a law banning billboards and I didn't to be associated with similar problems. But Lee was insistent. He wanted to take it before the board of directors and present it. I declined and told him that if he felt that strongly about it, that I would present it to the board."

As Gene anticipated, it was a tough sell. While the men who sat on the creamery's board were talented and shrewd, they were dairy farmers, not cartoon people. Their reaction was unanimous. They hated it.

"I explained that it was just an idea," Gene laughed years later. "I told them that we could try it and if it didn't work we could scrap it. I told them we would log any phone complaints and at the end of a month I'd report the results. We went round and round – they all wanted a real cow – but finally they gave the okay."

Even the prophetic Levinger could not have imagined the result. From the first billboard on U.S. Highway 101 – which featured Clo's smiling face and the simple imploration; "Support you local cow … buy Clover milk …" Levinger's happy bovine was off and grinning.

"We had no idea that she would take off like she did," said Gene. "The public really embraced her. It even surprised Lee! Now Clo is like part of the family. It's almost like she's a real person."

Indeed, everywhere there is Clover milk there is Clo. Her toothy likeness adorns delivery trucks, product cartons and clothing. Children sleep with Clo dolls and watch her commercials on TV. Mothers hang pictures on refrigerators with Clo magnets and schedule soccer games and dental appointments on Clo calendars. There are Clo stickers, buttons, badges and pins. With her whimsical smile and fluttering eyebrows she passes out ice cream at county fairs and waves to adoring crowds from her personal float in civic parades.

Clo is the punster extraordinaire. From her ubiquitous billboards she dispenses justice from her seat on the Supreme Quart and arbitrates Clos calls at local sporting events. Culturally sensitive she is a bovine artist. In a distinguished career she has bared her toga-clad shoulders as Venus de Moolo, smiled impishly as the Moona Lisa, donned a rakish beret to daub the canvas as Claude Moonet and clipped her ear as an enigmatic Vincent Van-Clo. In the world of Moosic she has composed her own motif as Wolfgang Amadeus Moozart, frolicked with her herd in the Sound of Moosic and preformed a Wagnerian opus.

Over the years Clo has remained fashionable and au courant. For her many friends – both human and bovine - her fine line of designer Clos are in constant demand. Now in her thirty-fifth year her ardent votaries have installed her permanently as the queen of Sonoma Cownty and the Finest in her Field. When asked how much longer she can continue to tip Clo through our two lips, Gene smiled and quipped; "Who knows. It's never Clover till the fat lady sings and until that time our cups runneth Clover."

CLOVER-STORNETTA FARMS

The birth of a company. Original owners of Clover-Sornetta Farm. L to R: Bill Van Dam, Paul, Ross, Al Stornetta, Dan Benedetti, John Markunsen, and Gene Benedetti. Not shown: Gary Imm.

XXXVII

"For us profit was not a compelling motive … we all shared a commitment to honor and justice."

Gary Imm

On an early summer morning in 1977 the board of directors of the California Co-operative Creamery (the co-op had dropped Petaluma from its name in the early 1970's) sat in the upstairs boardroom in silence. Beyond the window the town lazed in the summer heat. Out in the pastures the cows chewed contentedly and waited for the afternoon breeze to drift in from the coast and cool them down for the evening milking.

Inside the air was tense. There was a motion on the floor. President Jack Dei called for a vote. One by one the members raised their hands. The ayes had it. The distribution rights to the creamery would be sold, and with it a part of Petaluma's history.

As the meeting adjourned for lunch, Gene got up and walked to his corner office in a daze. "My stomach was in knots," he recalled. "I remember saying to myself … This is my life … what will I do?"

The source of Gene's anguish had started two years earlier on August 22, 1975 at 1:42 am when the Petaluma Fire Department responded to an alarm at Western and Baker streets. Despite rolling four pumpers, a hook and ladder unit and an aerial ladder truck, the thirty-one firefighters who hustled to the scene were too late. By the time they arrived and got their equipment working, half of the creamery was engulfed in flames and the other half was about to go up as well.

"I was home from college and working the night shift in the butter room," remembered son Herm. "We were packing and stacking butter. One of the supervisors came in and told us that there was a fire, but not to worry and to keep on working. He assured us that they could control it. We kept on going for an hour or so and then Paul Ross, the plant manager came in. He told us they were evacuating the building. When we got outside it was horrible."

"I got the call in the middle of the night," said Dan grimly. "I called Dad and drove to his house. We drove into town together. In the distance we could see the fire illuminating the night sky. By the time we got there the bottling plant, the testing lab and the receiving area were in flames. It was awful. I remember Dad telling Chief Ellwood to forget the bottling plant and to try and save the rest of the building. As it turned out, that was a wise move. The plant was built in two sections separated by a breezeway. The main condenser and butter operation along with the corporate offices were on one side and the bottling facility on the other. When dad had Chief Ellwood abandon his efforts on the bottling plant it saved the rest of the facility.

"But I'll tell you," he concluded. "For a while, it looked like everything would burn."

Even in the middle of the night the news spread across town. Don Ramatici showed up to see what he could do.

"Thank God Don came down," said Gene. "I knew almost at once that the plant was gone. I realized that our customers were going to be without milk the next morning if we didn't do something fast. Don was good enough to open up his offices and let us use his phones. We called all of our customers and told them the plant was burning but that somehow we would make our deliveries. I knew we'd need help so I called my friends at Crystal in Sacramento."

Founded in 1901, the Crystal Cream and Butter Company was (and still is) a premier supplier of dairy products to northern California. The owner, Carl Hansen and his sons, Carl, Gerald and Ken were all friends of Gene's. When the call for help came they stepped forward.

"The people at Crystal were just magnificent," said Gene. "When I called they offered to help in any way they could. We diverted our morning trucks to their bottling plant in Sacramento. We sent a load of cartons with them. They bottled our entire order that morning and we never missed a beat. As terrible as the fire was, and believe me it was terrible, we did not miss one delivery or let one customer down. Our friends at Crystal made that possible. And so did our people. They all rose to the occasion."

Fighting skillfully and heroically, Chief Ellwood's men pumped over 300,000 gallons of water on the holocaust and managed to save half of the plant. By the time the sun rose over the hills, things were finally under control.

The effects of the fire were devastating. It was a civic, financial and psychological disaster. To Petalumians the creamery was more than just a business; it was an intrinsic part of community life. And now what had once been a monument to the success of the town lay in ruins, a pall of black smoke drifting above the sodden embers into the bright country sky.

With estimates to rebuild at an astronomical $3.6 million, the financial loss was staggering and put the creamery's board of directors in an impossible position.

"They just couldn't reach a decision," said Gene. "They deliberated for two years. All the while, we were having our milk bottled down in The City by Foremost. That was a hassle. Their performance left much to be desired. We even had to send our own guy, Paul Ross down there to straighten out their operation. Paul was a hell of a guy and did a great job, but the whole situation without a bottling plant was very difficult."

"And, he went on, "there was a lot of pressure on me. Every time there was a board meeting the press would be waiting for me to tell them what the decision was. I had to stall them for two years. I told the board that they had to make up their minds. I couldn't keep putting these guys off. All in all it was a very difficult time, for the board, for our townspeople, and for our customers."

Thus it was with a sense of relief that Gene walked toward his office that summer morning. At least now he could tell the press, who would surely be calling, what the board had decided. But like a clenched fist, the knot in his stomach still lingered and the question in his mind would not go away ... This is my life ... what will I do? In typical style he made his decision in a heartbeat.

"We usually had lunch sent in," he explained. "That way we could work through and not waste time. By the time I walked down the hall to my office and returned to eat - it could not have been more than five minutes - I'd made my decision. I walked in, sat down and told them that I'd like to buy the business. I didn't have a dime to my name. I had no idea how I was going to do it. But I'd made up my mind."

The Co-Op evolved from the clop of horse's hooves...

To the chug of engines...

To sleek tankers...

To the modern high-tech processing & bottle operation of today.

****

When the great Danish writer, Karen Blixen wrote "God made the world round so we would never be able to see too far down the road," she must have had Gene Benedetti in mind. At an age when most men see the soft glow of retirement on the horizon, he was willing to risk everything on the unknown.

"Dad was like that," said Herm. "He never looked too far into the future. He never worried about things that were beyond his control, and he was never afraid of what might come."

"I think that's why he never had any money," Herm went on. "Don't get me wrong, Dad always made a good living and he always took great care of us, but he spent nearly everything he made. Appearances were deceiving. He had a nice car, but it was the company's, not his. And we had a nice house but he owed a ton of money on in. None of that bothered him. He lived like there was no tomorrow. So in that regard, taking a business risk was consistent with his personality."

The distribution package that was for sale included the rights to the Clover brand name (including Clo the Cow), the existing customer base, and the company's home delivery routes and trucks. The board gave Gene two weeks to cobble together a deal.

"I went to every bank in town," Gene laughed years later. "Not a one would loan me a dime. They couldn't. I didn't have any collateral. I was trying to raise over a million dollars. No bank would loan me that kind of money. I couldn't blame them, but still it was a bit sobering."

But Gene had learned early the old Irish adage; if you want to have a friend you have to be a friend - and over the course of his life, he had been a friend to a great many people.

"In order for my plan to work," he said, "I needed to acquire a bottling facility and borrow enough money to buy the distribution package from the creamery. I went to see my old friends, the Stornetta's."

Al and Charlie Stornetta, two of the oldest and most respected dairymen in California, owned and operated the Stornetta Brothers Dairy. Astute, honest and very successful, they had sold their milk for years to their solid base of loyal customers in and around the historic towns of Sonoma and Napa.

"I'd known Al and Charlie for years," said Gene. "They were my friends. I struck a deal with them whereby I would lease their bottling plant and take over their customer base. I would pay them a flat sum. In exchange for that, they would turn over their accounts receivables to me, which, as it turned out, were equal to the sum that I was putting up. That meant that if I could collect those accounts, I was home free. For them it was a good deal because they'd get cash, keep their land and herd, have a place to sell their milk each day and also receive a monthly lease payment."

"We made out," he continued, "because we had a bottling facility, a supply of milk from their herd, their customer base and the accounts receivables, which I was confident I could collect because I knew all of Al's customers."

The deal with the co-op was less complicated. "All I had to do with them," said Gene, "was come up with the money to purchase the wholesale distribution rights. I went to see my friends, the Hansen's, at the Crystal Cream and Butter Company in Sacramento. They were good business people - very honest and I'd know them for years. Romayne "Bud" Roberts was their controller and consigliore. He helped me put a deal together with them. They agreed to loan me the cash to do the entire deal. It was not charity. It was a loan and I'd have to make payments or they'd take the business. But now I had the financing and was ready to go."

While all of this was going on, Gene put together his ownership team drawn from former co-op employees. In addition to himself and the Stornetta brothers, John Markunsen bought in as vice president and sales manager; Bill Van Dam as controller; Paul Ross the talented plant operator as production manager; oldest son Dan as a member of the marketing team; and Gary Imm. Gary had worked since his teen-age days at the co-op and was an expert in virtually all phases of the operation. "Gary was and still is like a son to me," said Gene. "It was wonderful to have him as an owner."

Each owner purchased shares in the new venture. "It was really something," recalled Dan with a grin. "I don't think any of us had any money. I know Dad and I didn't. Hell we had to put up the note on our homes just to raise the capital to buy in. Talk about risk!"

"But you know," he went on, "the risk never bothered Dad. He was more worried about his reputation among his friends. He didn't care about the money. He didn't want to let his friends down. The guys who were going to be working for us in the plant, all the drivers on the routes, those guys were all his friends and he didn't want to let them down. And he didn't want to let mom and us kids down either. He wanted to build a legacy to leave to us. It was a very gutsy move on his part."

Jim Leprino, Chairman of Leprino Foods – the largest manufacturer of mozzarella cheese in the world – and a friend and business associate of Gene's for over thirty years put it this way; "If you think about Gene's life and what he did for the farmers in the area, he could have just stayed at the co-op and grown with its expansion. But he went into that business with real energy on behalf of his family. He knew it would change the future for his kids. He could have had a comfortable life but he did it to leave something for his kids. I've always respected him for that."

****

Clover-Stornetta Farms Inc. opened for business on August 1, 1977. For Gene, it was exhilarating; ("It was the first time in my life I felt truly independent"), and offered a chance to build a legacy that reflected his personality and philosophy.

CEO Gary Imm: "To some our philosophy seems a bit corny and even unsophisticated … but to us it was simple. Gene brought us all together as former employees of the co-op. We had no real expectations other than survival. We all shared a commitment to honor and justice. As issues came up they were placed within this framework of honor and justice. There were many times we could have cheated - sometimes by simply doing nothing. But we were all parents so if we did cheat, how could we go home and raise honorable children? For us, profit was not a compelling motive. We just kept working hard and tried to be as fair as we could."

"Gary's exactly right," agreed Dan. "We ran the company based on the principles that we had lived by all of our lives - the things that my Dad had taught us all. All of the owners were the same kind of people - just good honest hard working family men. We all had an inner strength from our wives and families."

In the early years the company operated from three locations, the Stornetta ranch in Sonoma, where all the bottling was done, and two distribution centers, one in Santa Rosa and the other forty miles south in San Rafael. Facilitated by a strong brand name, the inestimable advertising power of Clo the Cow – who by this time was grinning at the public from every delivery truck in the fleet – and the aggressive marketing of John Markunsen's sales team, the company prospered. Although those first years were tough, Gene and his partners stuck to their basic philosophy. Take care of your people, never say no to the community, and make profit subordinate to customer service.

"I never recall Dad saying no to a charity," said Dan. "We gave whenever we could. We also sent Clo the Cow everywhere. I don't think there was, or is, a kid in the five county area who has not received an ice cream either at the fair or at school from Clo."

Clover-Stornetta Farms was a family business. Gene's son Herm, who had been working elsewhere when the company was formed, was hired to run the bottling plant at the Stornetta ranch. Recently married, he and his wife Marilyn (herself a rancher's daughter) moved into Stornetta's old ranch house.

"We were out there for six years," said Marilyn. "Herm was on call day and night. I'd wake up when the babies cried and he'd wake up when the phone rang. We'd run specials together. Some restaurant in Napa would run out of milk so Herm would load the crates in the car and I'd put our baby Michael in the car seat and we'd run the special out in the middle of the night. It was the only time we'd get together."

"That's true," laughed Dan's wife Anne. "I don't know how many specials I ran out to the coast in those years. But it was what we had to do so we did it."

"We never thought about it," said Marilyn. "Those guys all worked so hard. We knew they'd make it."

Gene held his people in the highest esteem, paying top wages, providing the best available benefits and constantly preaching: "Our people are our most important asset."

"Every year," said Dan, "Dad threw a big picnic for the employees. We still do it and it's still the best day of the year. We invite the whole company and their families. We have a big barbecue. We never have it catered. All of us owners and a small group of employee volunteers do all the cooking and we serve each person. We eat last. It's a great day. We have swimming and games for the kids, and of course Clo shows up and passes out ice cream. I'll tell you, there were years where we made no profit, but Dad still insisted on the picnic. Today, if I had to cut out the picnic, I think I'd close up the company. That's how much it means to all of us."

By 1984 the company was in a position to consolidate. The two distribution terminals in Santa Rosa and San Rafael were closed and although the Stornetta plant was still in operation, all distribution was moved to a leased facility in Petaluma.

"We moved into what originally had been a chicken processing plant, and then later was a Del Monte frozen food facility" said Dan. "We were able to negotiate a favorable lease with the Brody family who had owned the building for years. It was a much better arrangement. We were more efficient and were back home in Petaluma."

But the homecoming was not without challenges. In an attempt to streamline billing and inventory control the company purchased a new computer system. In a clerical environment based on manual order taking and invoicing, the cold precision of a mid 1980's computer was a change that produced a set of problems that no one anticipated.

"It was a complete disaster," said Dan. "We'd finally gotten our company together. We'd moved back home, we'd consolidated to be more efficient and then the computer problems. We couldn't take a proper order, we couldn't generate an accurate invoice, and we couldn't bill for our product or collect any money. We lost complete internal control of the company. It happened so fast that by the time we realized what was going on we were on the edge of bankruptcy. What was really scary was that no one knew how to fix it."

Enter Gary Imm. Born and reared in Petaluma, Gary spent the summers of his youth bucking hay and working on local ranches. After graduating from Petaluma High School in 1963 he married his high school sweetheart Lynn Holmes, and went to work for Gene at the Co-op. A dynamic man with an uncommon work ethic, Gary knew every job in the business except milking the cows - and if need be he'd tackle that. When the company's internal mechanisms crumbled, he knew what to do.

"I called everyone together," he recalled years later. "I knew what they were going through. At one time or another I had held all of their jobs. People were just giving up. I asked them to put all of the issues on the table so they could vent their frustrations. I asked them to stop pointing fingers, and convinced them to not give up. I asked them to give me a month."

"Not surprisingly," he went on, "the problem was a lack of communication. For example, we moved in June and a few months later school started. That's a big time of year for us because the schools order large quantities of milk for the kids. We'd get an order for 20,000 ½ pints of milk from some school district and the next week someone would hit an additional '0' on the computer and the same customer would order 200,000 ½ pints. The guy pulling the order in the cooler would go nuts, the loader would wonder how to get it in the truck and the driver would wonder what the hell was going on! In the meantime the computer would spit out an invoice. Naturally the school would dispute it and hold up payment. The whole thing was just a nightmare."

Dairying is a dynamic business; cows produce milk twice a day so it was impossible to shut down operations to reorganize. It was like rebuilding an engine while it was still running. With a clear eye on the problem, Gary called the computer programmers together.

"Look," he told them. "For a customer to bump up their order by 100% in a week is not reasonable. The system has to catch that or we'll never get this under control."

When the computer people responded that their machines had no concept of "reason" and were only capable of spewing out what was put in. Gary answered with a stroke of practical genius.

"I had them program the computer to generate a weekly report that told me if there was a discrepancy of 15% or more on any account. I called it a "Reasonability Report" and we still run it today. It solved the problem. Now if a customer's order was out of whack, if it wasn't reasonable, I'd know about it at once, and we could make adjustments. Before long we were back on track and the problems went away."

"I'll tell you right now," said Dan, "Gary Imm saved our company. You have to understand it was like going into a hornets' nest and organizing the hornets. He couldn't just shut things down and start over. He totally reorganized the internal infrastructure of our company on the fly. It was brilliant. Without him we would have lost the company and gone bankrupt. It was that close. Gary is a genius."

But internal challenges notwithstanding the vicissitudes of the marketplace would soon threaten to sweep Gene and his partners' company away.

****

There are few activities in the human experience more intimate or necessary than eating. In the years when America was a nation of small town's food was a local experience. Indeed when Evelyn Benedetti shopped for groceries at Baccala's corner market, it's a safe bet that the poultry, meat and dairy products she purchased were grown on family ranches a few miles from her kitchen door.

But as the country became increasingly urbanized all of that changed. The corner Mom and Pop stocked by local suppliers all but disappeared and was replaced by the corporate supermarket full of commodities packaged and promoted by Madison Avenue. In a country of nearly 300 million people the food business became a $450 billion a year industry catering to consumers with little concern and less knowledge about where their food came from. Milk was no exception.

But Clover-Stornetta Farms held a different view. Firmly believing that the personality and philosophy of their company, and the climate and culture of their region made their products superior, they were convinced that, if called upon, their customers would remain loyal.

In the mid-1980's their convictions were challenged when two industry giants, Foremost and Knudsen went head-to-head in an attempt to capture the dairy market in Northern California. Their tactics were predatory and simple; drive the wholesale price of milk so low that the other guy either goes under, or goes home.

For small companies like Clover-Stornetta, the situation was potentially disastrous. The effects were immediate when long time customer, Roger Wilco Markets – a Novato based independent chain – adopted a "milk is milk" posture and replaced Clover-Stornetta in its stores.

"They were a great store and a fine customer" said Dan. "But what could they do? They called dad and said they were taking us out of their stores. We knew we had a serious problem because we simply could not compete in price. For us it was the beginning of the end. We were done."

Gene's response was courageous and emphatic: "We will not move off of our price, he said. "We cannot afford to. We have taken care of our customers and our community for all of these years. They will take care of us."

"I thought we were finished," said Dan. "I thought we'd lose our customers one by one. But Dad was right. A couple of weeks after they removed our milk the guy called us back. He told us that people had stopped coming into his stores! They just stopped! They wouldn't shop there because there was no Clover-Stornetta milk on the shelves. He said his stores were empty. He put our milk back in the next day."

A similar incident took place in a more emotional environment when a local school district awarded their milk contract to the lowest bidder and removed Clover from its schools. To their chagrin, district officials discovered that the fury of a woman scorned paled in comparison to that of a group of mothers who were loathe to feed their children anything other than Clo the Cows nectarous milk. The ensuing revolt and protest at the next school board meeting persuaded officials to quickly reinstate Clover.

"When things like that happened," Dan said proudly, "we knew we had something special. We learned that Dad had been right. If we put our people, our customers and our community first, they would be loyal to us and take care of us. Dad knew it all the time. But we had to learn it – and we did."

BACK TO THE FUTURE

Three generations of family ownership. Back row, L to R: John Markunsen, Herm Benedetti, Dan Benedetti, Kevin Imm. Front row, L to R: Gary Imm, Gene Benedetti, and Mike Keefer.

XXXVIII

"Treat the earth well: it was not given to you by your parents, it was loaned to you by your children. We do not inherit the earth from our ancestors, we borrow it from our children."

Ancient Indian Proverb

In 1992 Clover-Stornetta Farms celebrated its fifteenth year of operations. What had started as an idea born of the ashes of uncertainty was now a thriving business that, like its antecedent, had become a deeply woven part of community life. By this time Gene had stepped back from the day-to-day operations of the business to assume a position as Chairman of the Board. Oldest son Dan had stepped in as President, Gary Imm as Chief Executive Officer and second son Herm as Vice of President of Human Resources.

"They are all good men," said Gene. "They were ready to run the company and it was very satisfying to turn it over to them. John Markunsen is a life long friend, his son-in-law Mike Keefer is like a son. Paul Ross is another great friend. And Gary's son Kevin

– I just can't say enough about all of the fine men who were more than fellow owners – they were like brothers to me."

A long-term lease had been negotiated and a new bottling and processing plant (designed by Gary Imm) had been built – the heart of which was the high-speed bottling line manufactured by the Tetra Pack Company of Sweden. Gary built a ramp and large viewing window for visitors and the many school children who came to take a tour, enjoy a free ice cream and see the home of Clo the Cow.

"The new line increased our production to the point where we could shut down the Sonoma plant," explained Dan. "Now our entire operation was home in Petaluma, where we belonged."

Under the creative guidance of Jim Benefield, who had purchased the Levinger advertising agency, Clo the Cow's toothy grin became even more ubiquitous, not only appearing throughout the Redwood Empire but also on Clover trucks that made daily deliveries in The City and to towns as far south as Monterey.

"Dad was invaluable to us in those years," said Herm. "He became like an ambassador. He knew so may people and helped us with his connections and friends. He was the steward of our heritage and we always knew we could rely on him. "

"I agree," said Dan. "He was, and still is a great advisor. We faced many challenges in those years and Dad's wisdom and advice was indispensable."

But in an era when national corporations were consolidating the industry, surviving as an independent was a precarious proposition and the enticement to sell was an ever-present temptation.

"By the mid-1990's the business had become very successful," Gene said. "The boys came to me and told me they'd received an offer to sell out. The numbers were huge. They could have retired as rich men. But I told them that I'd vote against it. We – and when I say we I mean they - had built a business that was very special - not only to them, but also to their community. I told them that keeping the business was the greatest thing they could do. All they would get if they sold was money. And what good was that if they didn't do good things with it?"

"It was tempting for us all," said Dan. "But Dad was right. We knew we'd built a good company. But the milk processing business is so competitive that something had to happen to set us apart. We just didn't know what that something would be."

That something came in the form of Recombinant Bovine Somatotropin better known as rBST. Introduced in the early 1990's by the Monsanto Corporation, rBST is a veterinary drug derived from a protein produced in the pituitary glands of cows. When injected into lactating cattle it can increase milk production by up to fifteen percent. For a product as nondescript as milk, where volume is measured by hundred weight, and profit margins are calculated in pennies, it was the best thing since the automatic milking machine.

"You have to understand," explained Dan. "Milk is a pretty unexciting product. There is not much you can say about it except it's fresh and cold. Nobody ever tried to say they had the 'best' milk because no one really knew what the 'best' milk was. It was white and came from cows. That was about it. Most people felt that an additive that increased production was a great thing."

But not everybody felt that way.

"Our customer base is very well educated, very affluent and extremely health conscious," said Dan. "It's like nowhere else in the United States. When they discovered that Clover cows would be injected with the growth hormone rBST they voiced their displeasure. That and a concern that it might harm the animals put us in a real dilemma. We knew we had to respond to our customers and we did not want to participate in anything that might be hurting our producer's cattle. Our choices were to keep the status quo or to try something new. We chose the latter."

Drawing from a database of over 150 candidates Dan and his partners formed an elite consortium of sixteen local dairies dedicated to producing the finest, cleanest, most wholesome milk possible. Called North Coast Excellence (NCE) it was a tough club to join. NCE members were required to produce milk that not only exceeded federal guidelines in cleanliness (measured in coliform counts, standard plate counts and somatic cell counts) but were also prohibited from injecting their cattle with rBST. Moreover, following guidelines established by the University of California at Berkeley, NCE members were required to embrace the concept of sustainable agriculture and practice methods that made their operations economically viable, socially responsible and environmentally sound. And finally, each member had to maintain a beautiful ranch.

"We found that the best milk tends to come from the nicest looking ranches," explained Dan. "All of our producers keep the most beautiful ranches imaginable. We are proud to suggest to our customers that they drive out and see the green open pastures, white fences, beautiful homes, well ventilated barns and happy cows that make their milk."

"Every year," Dan continued, "we have a CPA firm come in and audit the program to keep us on track. So far it's worked beautifully. It has allowed us to maintain total control over where our milk comes from. We test each load from each herd every day.

Just like the old days, our customers know exactly where their milk comes from."

"And," he went on, "the program has restored incentive for our producers. When they were producing for a co-op, it did not matter how good their milk was. Now it does. Our producers are fantastic people. They are a collection of wonderful families. Many of them are third generation ranchers. They stepped up and took the incentive to be progressive, to constantly improve and to make the best product available. It has been said that we make the cleanest milk in the world. I don't know if we do or not. But I'll guarantee you, if it's not, it's pretty darn close!"

In early 1998 Clover-Stornetta took their program to a higher level when they partnered with NCE member Saint Anthony Farms and entered the burgeoning organic market.

Founded in San Francisco in 1950 by Franciscan Friar Alfred Boeddeker, the Saint Anthony Foundation is dedicated to enhancing the inherent dignity of each person. Their motto; "To feed, heal, shelter, clothe, lift the spirit of those in need, and create a society in which all persons flourish … " was a perfect fit for the Clover-Stornetta family.

Operating as a residential drug and alcohol recovery program on a lovely 315-acre farm near Petaluma, Saint Anthony's residents milk a herd of about 200 cattle fed on a diet of 100% organically grown feed. With its lush green pastures, pristine white fences and well kept and modern milking barn, Saint Anthony's is an enchantingly beautiful environment for its once disenfranchised residents to live, work, and through the counsel and skill of their mentors, learn to take responsibility for their lives.

"We could not have asked for a better organic partner than Saint Anthony's," Dan exclaimed. "They truly do produce the

'Milk of Human Kindness.'"

As the new millennium approached, the North Coast Excellence program and their relationship with Saint Anthony's had made Clover-Stornetta Farms a local celebrity in the dairy business.

"We did stand apart," admitted Dan. "But to us it was just a natural response to the needs of our customers and our producers. To us they are family. Quite honestly, we never expected to be recognized beyond our local area. When the American Humane Association contacted us we were completely surprised."

Established in 1877 the American Humane Association (AHA) has long advanced their mission to prevent cruelty and exploitation of children and animals. Holding strong to their noble vision of a society in which no child or animal is victimized by abuse or neglect, the AHA got word of Clover-Stornettas' model program. After conducting their own certification process, they concluded that Clover-Stornetta Farms deserved to be the first and only dairy in the United States to receive their coveted Free Farmed label for humanely produced animal products. The distinction brought the company national recognition and was a jeweled capstone to a business dedicated to the welfare of its people, the satisfaction of its customers, the safety of its animals and the conservancy of the environment.

But in a more prescient sense these encomiums and recognition bore a greater message. They were a tangible extension of the values and philosophy that Gene had learned from his parents who, on that day so long ago, had planted their feet on their own land and committed themselves to nurture, respect and keep it forever.

"You know,' said Gene. "Over the years people have come to me and told me that I was a 'throwback'. That the way we ran our lives and business was something from the distant past. But to me it has never been like that. I just did the things my parents taught me to do and tried to pass those things on to my kids. A throwback? No. I think we are a model."

EPILOGUE

Gene and Evie, my Godparents.

"Some of its magic and some of its tragic,
but I've had a great life all the way."

From He Went to Paris
By Jimmy Buffett

On a late August day in 2003 I drove north across the fog-sheeted Golden Gate, passed through the Waldo Tunnel and emerged into the bright sunlight of Marin County. As I drove through the valleys – burned maize by the summer sun - the circean towns of Clover Country rushed by; Sausalito, Tiburon, San Rafael, Novato, then out onto the flat Santa Rosa plain, up the grade to Petaluma and on to Cotati where I pulled off the highway into the foothills outside town. Off Poplar Avenue I turned down the familiar driveway, made my way up to the big house and parked once more under the great eucalyptus tree. Inside the house my Godfather waited. Like Saint Luke's parable of the prodigal son, his joy and affection upon seeing me was unconditional. We fixed a drink and sat at the wooden table like we'd done so many times before.

"It's good to have you back, Buck."

"It's good to be back."

I was home.

Later that afternoon, Gene and Evelyn gathered us all on the tree-shaded patio for drinks and barbecue and to enjoy the relaxed acceptance of the family. Beyond the western mountains, the sun sank into the sea and splashed a last flush of summer light.

We moved inside to sit for supper and my Godfather asked me to return the blessing. We joined hands and bowed our heads.

"Dear God," I prayed. "Thank you for this family. Thank you for the countless times you have brought us together in this house to enjoy your bounty. Bless all in this house. Keep them healthy and safe, that we may enjoy their fellowship and their laughter. Thank you for your enduring countenance among us. Keep us humble and keep us grateful. Amen."

Outside the open window a quiet wind ruffled through the vineyard and brought with it the everlasting smell of the land. When we were finished I looked up and smiled at my Godparents, and, like all who have known this wonderful couple and their family, my heart was filled - cum benedictis - with blessings.

Doug Pricer and his Godfather, Gene Benedetti.